Eph 4:1-2
— Kim Combes

Walk In A Manner Worthy

A Voice In The Foster & Adoptive Care Wilderness

By M. Kim Combes, M.Ed

First Edition   © 2020

Table of Contents

Biography 1

Endorsements 2

Acknowledgements 3

Foreward 10

Preface 12

Introduction 16

Safety Issues: Reflections of 9/11 18

Kinship Care 20

Post Adoption Dilemmas 22

Legislation Opportunities 24

Foster/Adoptive Care Training 27

Just 1 Person by Travis Lloyd 31

Educating Foster and Adoptive Parent
(and Those With Whom They Work) 36

What Kids Need to Get "Past the Past" 39

A Letter Written to My Friend, Bryan Post 43

Parenting With Pizazz 45

Ignorance Isn't Always Bliss 48

A View From the Zoo 50

The Importance of Biological Family in Foster Care/Adoption ... 53

Connecting With Birth Parents 56

Father's Day Letter 60

Table of Contents

Adverse Childhood Experiences 62
If You Only Knew What I Know 64
We Can All Make A Difference 66
A Birthday Blessing 68
Journey With Jason 72
JoJo's Story 76
Darrin's Story 80
COMBEZ Inn 84
Self-Injurious Behavior: A Cutter's Story 94
Self-Injurious Behaviors: Help Stop The Pain 97
Who Will Cry 102
Only In My Dreams 106
James' Testimony 108
Letter From Adam 112
No Regrets 115
As A Foster Parent 119
God's Kisses On The Forehead 121
The Black Dot 126
Little Annie 131
My Worst "Best" Christmas Ever 133
Speaking Endorsements 136
Vita For Mr. Kim Combes, M.Ed. 143

Walk In A Manner Worthy

Biography

Punny man, Kim Combes, M.Ed. hails from Colo, Iowa and has been employed in various capacities of the human service arena since 1980. From youth counselor/therapist in residential treatment facilities to an Iowa Department of Human Services social worker (and current director of Combes Counseling and Consultation), Kim has ministered to myriad struggling children and families. Too, he and Diane, his wife of 21 years, have adopted five children with special needs, now all adults.

Throughout his career, Kim has enjoyed serving on various boards and committees, such as that of the National Foster Parent Association and the Iowa Foster Adoptive Parent Association. His hobbies include spending time with family and friends, writing, reading, traveling, preparing/eating unique food recipes and conjuring up all forms of PUNS for his play-on-words Facebook fans.

Kim is a popular national trainer and has, over the course of the last quarter century, presented cutting-edge materials on trauma as well as multiple techniques to assist in the healing of the hearts of challenging children. Target audiences include foster/adoptive parents, social workers/counselors, teachers, day care providers and anyone else wanting to hone skills to help all children thrive.

One would also find Kim actively involved in local church activities with a focus on mentoring young men in progressive stages of their Christian journey. It is his greatest desire to one day hear from his Lord and Savior "Well done, good and faithful servant."

Endorsements

Kim Combes, impressive book! Your vast range of experiences in the foster care system provide compassion and honesty as you described some of the many memories you share of the good, the great, the bad and the ugly all rolled into one. This is a true and accurate description of foster care and why we love this incredibly difficult, yet incredibly rewarding work, whether it be by staff as their job or by volunteers as foster caregivers. Vera Fahlberg once said that "every child deserves an irrational advocate." You, kind sir, definitely meet her criteria!.
Irene Clements, President of the National Foster Parent Association

---

However you parent a child, whether as a foster or adoptive parent, birth parent, grandparent, or other, this is one book that you will want on your shelf. Kim Combes provides important insight into the challenges that parents face today in a personal and powerful way. This book is one that will not only educate you, but also inspire and motivate you. It is an honest look at parenting from a Christian perspective that will stir great emotion in you.
Dr. John DeGarmo, Director of The Foster Care Institute

I have always known Kim Combes to be a remarkable storyteller, with each of his personal reflections focused on truth, humor and the power of love. This compendium is an uplifting collection of Kim's stories designed to inspire and instruct parents and all others who touch the lives of children.
Heather Craig-Oldsen, Professor Emerita/Former Social Worker/Child Welfare Consultant

---

It was with great pleasure that I was able to pre-read and comment on Kim's book "Walk in A Manner Worthy: A Voice in the Foster/Adoptive Care Wilderness". Each chapter gives you a glimpse into the lives of a foster/adoptive parent and/or a foster/adoptive child. Each chapter provides a learning experience that can be researched more or applied to your situation. This book is not a textbook study, but instead real life experiences of one who has been there. A must read!
Lynhon Stout, Social Worker/Former Executive Director of the Iowa Foster and Adoptive Parent Association

Endorsements

Kim is passionate and determined in helping the children and other foster/adoptive parents. His emotion and compassion drives his ability to teach others about the trials and tribulations of parenting children who have experienced trauma. He has used his story telling technique to help hundreds of people to keep pushing through the difficult times and make a lifelong impact on the children. People who have attended his training sessions continue to remember and use the lessons they have learned years later.
Denise Gibson, MA, Former Director and Consultant of an International Foster/Adoptive Parent Program

---

What a blessing to have known Kim Combes for many years as a friend, as a partner in many areas relating to foster care and adoption issues. We have attended many conferences, workshops, meetings throughout the country and I have even visited in the Combes home. Kim and his wife, Diane, have always been models to other foster/adoptive parents, by their own experiences.

I feel Kim has stepped up to another level in his authoring this book. With his experiences, his knowledge and his desire to help others, I am proud to be given this opportunity to be included. I know that God will bless all his efforts and certainly, I wish him the best. He is well deserving of this opportunity.
Betty Daigle Hastings, Author/Trainer-Presenter/"Mom"

"He who hardens his heart to the cry of the poor, will also cry out himself and not be heard." (Proverbs 21:13)

Kim Combes is certainly not a person who has hardened his heart to the cry of the poor! I recognized his soft heart as we interacted at various junctures in the foster/adoption journey we were both traveling. As we sped along the pathway, we chatted about our stumblings, successes and profound missteps. I remember hearing Kim lament the $2500 phone bill to porn numbers his sweet challenges had run up and I quipped "You know you can block those numbers, don't you?" He said, "I know now!" Only another foster parent can relate and laugh afterwards.

Kim has an unusual heart for the wayward youth in our communities who need structure, boundaries, unwavering love and acceptance, no matter what. Many of these young men, now grown, know that Kim is in their corner, rooting for them and pointing them to the Father who sees all, knows all and faithfully loves.

With gratitude, I highly recommend this book (and this author) to you for your encouragement in helping youth along their journey to productive adulthood.
Elaine Cox RN (retired), Foster-Adoptive Parent with lots of gray hair too.

Acknowledgements

As Mr. Foxhoven so astutely points out in his forward to this book, "Kim Combes is not a solo act." This project would not be in existence had it not been for myriad people whose lives have, directly and indirectly, influenced mine by giving generously of their time, talent, support, prayers and even from their bank account. I would be greatly remiss if I did not give them honor for all they have done for me.

This book has been several years in the making. Only God could have made this possible via the contributions given by those I'm about to mention. I apologize in advance for not being able to give thanks to all who might have contributed said support to accomplish the completion of this work.

First, thank you to four decades of clients who shared their lives with me during seasons of great heartache for them. They inadvertently honored me by sharing their brokenness – trusting me to the degree they could given the hurt, shame and guilt they felt for having me, a social worker, in their lives. I know it was humbling for them to admit need in the stressful situations that lead to my becoming involved. Their determination to survive (and thrive) in the tumultuous waves of grief and loss was phenomenal. And certainly kudos to all the young men with whom I shared my home since 1994 when I took the step of faith to the assignment I believe God called me to…that of being a foster parent. It's been a rollercoaster ride, but I appreciate all I learned while sharing life, as hard as it was sometimes for all of us.

Thanks go to Jerry, Irene, John, Heather, Denise, Lynhon, Betty and Elaine for the forward and endorsements written to plug my project. Given the respect and admiration I have for all of you, I actually got teary as I read them. You have no idea how much your words mean to me. And that goes, also, for those who gave rave reviews of my training presentations which are towards the back of this book; all priceless to me.

I asked Jill King, a Facebook friend whom I'd met only once, to be my editor. She agreed for a very reasonably set price. To my surprise, after reading and editing my manuscript, she wouldn't take the money. She told me to give it to a good cause, which I did. I sent it to my Pakistani "sons" in the Lord, Aqib John and Pastor Adil, who, too, have been praying for the success of this book.

Much appreciation to all those involved in the FOSTERING FAMILIES TODAY magazine. Many of the stories you will read in this book were first published in the pages of this periodical. Advance thanks to Kim Hansel, editor, for the review she

Walk In A Manner Worthy

reported she would do when this project is completed.

Among the articles you are about to read are those written by other people who have agreed to contribute to the "wilderness" storyline. Honorable mentions go to James Nieman, Joseph "JoJo" Kope, Adam Henderson, Travis Lloyd and Julianne Faas for their submissions and contributions to my life. Thank you.

Who doesn't want generous friends with a lakeside home? Much gratitude goes to Loren and Darla Winkelhorst for their willingness to let me stay at Lake Okoboji for a week so I could write, organize, relax and enjoy complete solitude. That September week was the sunniest, warmest 7 days of that particular autumn season. What a gift from God. Thank you, college friends, for this experience.

Special thanks to my Church family everywhere for prayers, encouragement and love. Locally, I want to call out Cornerstone Church of Christ in Zearing, Iowa. These siblings in Jesus highly impacted me for two decades plus. So many poured into my broken life and loved me over many years. Thanks also to Harvest Vineyard Church in Ames, for a new season of fellowship, continued growth and healing. Many of you prophesied over me regarding this book, not knowing that several others were prompted to give me the same exact message. I guess God wanted me to "get it". Extra thanks to Burt, Daniel and David Blom, Teri and Don Thompson, Ruo-Qi Wright, Lori Voss-Siders, Jerry Floyd, Chuck Ryan, Gene Wiley, Harley Osborn, Kent Prescott and several others, including our ever-evolving Tuesday night home group that kept prodding me to get this done when fear and doubt hindered any future progress. Your prayers kept me moving forward. I am eternally grateful. Love you guys.

How does one express so much appreciation to mentors one has never personally met? Two men I feel bonded with who don't know me from Adam. Loud shout outs to Mark Batterson (Lion Chasers) and John Eldredge (Wild at Heart) who have impacted my life in ways they will never know. I admire these Christian authors so much and wanted them to get credit for how much influence they have had over me in accomplishing this formidable task. If I don't ever get to say THANK YOU in person on this side of eternity, I most assuredly will on the other side.

To Linda Fries, the artist who designed the cover – what can I say? You've been my Christian Mom since I was 18 years old, letting me share life - laughing, praying, crying, and growing together in different seasons of our faith journey. Your generosity in allowing me to use your art means more than you'll know. I didn't know when

Acknowledgements

I chose it from your collection that you had entitled it "Home". What a confirmation from God that this was it. Thank you for all you've done for me since we met in Spring of 1976. I will cherish our friendship into eternity walking hand in hand with our mutual Lord, Savior and Risen King, Jesus Christ. Blessings, dear friend.

Hitchhiking off gratitude for Linda, I have to mention Gary Banzer-Holland, a Portland, Oregon photographer who graciously gave me a good price to venture out to Linda's relative to whom she had given this painting. Gary took such amazing care in capturing it digitally that Paul could then make it into this cover successfully. Thank you, Gary. May your business thrive.

And to Paul Oyen, my spiritual brother who has dedicated multiple free hours of time and talent to get this manuscript into book form. I could never have done this without your skilled hand and knowledge of how to format for final publication. May the Lord bless you abundantly for your efforts to make this project a success for the eternal Kingdom.

Mark Batterson, whom I've previously mentioned, taught me through his writings not to seek the solution to whatever problem I might face, but to seek whole-heartedly, and with praise, the Solution-Giver, which I did regarding funding for this book. It is human nature to question and doubt God when faced with what seems like insurmountable odds against hope of problem solving. I am rich in friends and blessings, but not so much concerning finances. Enter my friend, who wishes to remain nameless. Long story short, my friend and I knew OF each other years before actually meeting. He had been praying for an older man, a Paul if you will, that would come into his life to mentor him as a husband, father and man of God. I didn't know that I would soon be the answer to that prayer. In meeting the first time, just short of three hours, we connected on a level that only God could have made happen. We talked and prayed, even got teary some as we shared life stories. Now, enter God. As we were ending our time together, my friend blurted "God just told me that I am to fund your book up to $10,000." "What did you say?" "You heard me." I wept, overwhelmed with sheer joy for how God answered my need as I pursued HIM, not the solution to my money deficit. So....dear friend and brother in Christ, this book is yours...and God's, of course. Since that day 18 months ago, life has been interesting to say the least. But know how thankful I am to God for a Timothy like you. I am honored to be your friend, your brother, your Paul. Many blessings to you and your family, my son in the Lord.

Walk In A Manner Worthy

Nicole, Matt, Jose, Destiney, Jordan and Logan... know that I love you. You all know I am anything but perfect, but know that I am hopeful that, while not biologically related to any of you, I have reflected Jesus to you in a way that convinces you that as a dad, through all our trials and tribulations, you are loved greatly by God, by Mom and me and by others who know you. I've learned so much from you, all of which invites me to be a better man. THANK YOU for sharing your lives with us.

Justin, Elijah, Silas and baby Mila – you are all greatly loved. I love being Grandpa. Know that I will pray for all of you until God takes me Home. And I'm covering your parents in prayer too, just so you know.

And to Diane, my wife, whom God has given me. You have loved me through everything the last twenty one years of our marriage. I am the first to admit I am a bit tough to love some days (understatement, I know). I have my own wounds, my own issues after decades of working with pain and dysfunctional lives in the human service arena. Sometimes I feel like I've got my own "reactive attachment disorder" due to vicarious trauma. Through fostering teen boys, adopting five kids each with their own special needs, through grief, hurts and sorrows, you have stuck by me, supporting me, praying for me, crying with me and, at times, *because* of me. I am thankful to our Lord for how He's grown both of us in our journey of faith. I don't want to do this life without you. Thank you for your love, prayers and constant support through thick and thin. As scripted in our wedding rings, "One day at a time" whatever comes our way. Love you.

While both are gone now, I want to thank my parents, Donna and Tom, who loved and raised me years ago. We didn't always see things eye-to-eye over the years, but my work in the career field I chose made me realize how blessed I was to have you as parents. You did the best you knew how, given many life obstacles, to shape me into the man I've become. I would like to think you'd be proud of all that God has done in and through me. And to Virla and Duane Caskey (now passed also), thank you for raising my wife to have a heart for others and for all you've done for both of us over the years. Mom Virla, you're the only one left now. Know that we love you very much.

And last but certainly not least, thank you Father God/Lord Jesus for calling my name back on Christmas Day 1975. You have blessed me above and beyond anything I could have ever asked or even imagined. May this project bring you much glory, for that is indeed my intent – to point readers to You. May these writings encourage, inspire and spur readers to good works and deeds and, of course, to

Acknowledgements

Yourself. Please whisper their names as they read these "slices of life" so they, too, will know how much You love them.

PS God, thank you for the title of this book. And for those of you who have read up to this point, here's the rest of the story.

I was reading through the entire book of Ephesians every day in March 2019. I had just read the first three chapters when I took the last gulp of that cup of my morning java. Getting a refill, my thoughts flitted to the topic of this project. I stared out the kitchen window into the pre-dawn darkness, asking God for a title of my book. I heard in my head "It will be Biblical". I laughed out loud. "Well, God, that certainly narrows it down." I sat back down to finish Ephesians, starting with chapter 4. As I read, part of the first verse literally got bold print and jumped up off the page, just a tad. "I, therefore, the prisoner of the Lord, entreat you to WALK IN A MANNER WORTHY to the calling with which you have been called..."

I thus had my title. It was shortly thereafter the remaining part came to mind. I pray the "voice" will influence many for good...and for God.

Walk In A Manner Worthy

Foreward by Jerry Foxhoven

Kim Combes is a man of extraordinary humor, compassion, perseverance and faith. All of this shows in this collection of writings. Kim relates his first-hand experiences as a foster parent and youth advocate in a way that grabs the reader. His writing is, above all else, authentic. He pulls no punches in this work. He talks about his successes as well as his failures. He examines the supreme joys of working with foster youth and their families in his journey as a foster parent, as well as his disappointments in the same journey. He has learned many lessons along the way, and he freely shares those lessons with the reader in this collection.

While the issue of faith does not dominate this work, it is certainly a thread that is weaved throughout. Much the way that faith weaves throughout Kim's life, it weaves through the writings that are collected here. Make no mistake: this is not a religious work. However, one cannot question the fact that Kim's faith has been at the core of why he became a foster parent and why he made so many sacrifices to serve the youth and families with whom he came in contact. Kim has a higher purpose for what he does, and it is that higher purpose that often helps him survive the disappointments and celebrate the successes. He is mission-driven.

If the reader is a foster parent, these writings will not only inspire but also instruct. Kim has learned a lot in his decades of service as a foster parent and trainer, and he freely shares the lessons that he has learned in these writings. If the reader is a social worker or child advocate, this book will provide great insight into the needs and challenges facing advocates who promote improvements in the child welfare system. If the reader is neither of these, the readings can be equally inspiring and instructive. All of these writings help the reader understand what it is to be human.

Even more importantly, this collection of writings is just plain fun. They will make the reader smile, laugh and, at times, cry. The writings progress through Kim's journey and the reader can see a maturity that develops in the attitude of the author as he experiences the joys and the disappointments of working with challenging youth and families. In the end, there is no other conclusion than that Kim Combes is a better person because of his experiences as a foster parent and as a child and family advocate. It is also inescapable that the commitment, compassion and determination of people like Kim Combes (as evidenced in these writings) make the world a better place.

Acknowledgements

Kim Combes is not a solo act: he is not the only person out there doing great work to support youth and families. However, he is a great example of what is possible when a strong faith is combined with compassion, and these writings show what is possible. Enjoy.

Jerry Foxhoven, Former Director Iowa Department of Human Services.

Preface

Welcome to my story. The genesis of this book actually goes back to 1973 when my Freshman English teacher assigned us a paper on a topic of our choice, minimum 15 typewritten pages (no computers). I had just finished reading a book about Albert Fish, an infamously known serial killer. As the author delved into Fish's psyche and his subsequent bizarre behaviors, this biography caused me to contemplate deeply the "why" of such conduct. I seemed at that time to be drawn into the darkness of human complexities and thus I chose MENTAL HEALTH as my topic of choice.

An average student, not then given towards exploring the format of the written word, I initially struggled with putting pen to paper, but once engaged I gave my all. Not only did I double the number of assigned pages, I, unbeknownst to me at the time, cracked open the door to my future.

Upon graduation from Westmar College in 1980, having majored in psychology and sociology, I accepted my first job in the human service arena at a residential treatment facility in Ames, Iowa. This facility housed 14 youngsters with emotional/behavioral issues, some of whom had no family for which to return when once graduated from the program. This 3-year stint with these troubled children was thus my foray into the world of alternative home placements.

The past 4 decades in this field have stretched me in ways that I could never have imagined. Residential counselor. Educational aide. State social worker. Training developer. In-home therapist. Community services specialist. Private agency therapist. Foster and adoptive parent. National presenter. Each hat I wore, coupled with the corresponding responsibilities in the aforementioned capacities, blurred one into another creating a stepping stone effect into even higher levels of responsibility and knowledge – to the degree that sometimes these roles completely overlapped. It was no easy task being employed as an in-home worker serving area-wide foster families while then simultaneously having to return to my own home to tackle foster parent duties of my own.

There were significantly dark days challenging me to wonder if I was making even an iota of a difference in the lives of others. On the other end of the emotional continuum, however, were days so filled with hope and joy abounding as I watched hurting families and children overcoming, against all odds, their particular challenges with so much grace I could only say "thank you, God" for allowing me to be a

Preface

part of their healing process. In retrospect, I realized I really had no idea what I was doing except that I longed to reflect my Christian values to members of a hurting culture, showing them the dignity and respect due them regardless of their choices or lot in life.

The journey has had many a rocky road, but I've met some absolutely phenomenal people along the way – people who have honored me by sharing their heart, trusting me to have unconditional positive regard toward them through all their tears, fears and deep emotions. Too, they allowed me the opportunity to grow, to think outside the box while always unknowingly inviting me to be the best I was meant to be also. Many of those same people helped me to see things in them – and in myself – that would have otherwise perhaps stayed buried, but in the surfacing brought the relief of freedom from the slavery of bondage, i.e. poor self-esteem and myriad other onerous yokes universal to the human condition.

The project you now hold in your hands was borne of countless tears and sleepless nights, an undertaking of great effort and no small amount of energy. I cannot, even as the author, take much credit for what you're about to read, however. The words are simply a diary, if you will, of a plethora of mutual experiences and overwhelming encouragement from those who saw in me what I could not see in myself. Any gifts you glean that I might have are only a sum total of what God has done in and through me utilizing my sphere of influence to provide me way more wisdom and support than I believe I ever doled back to those in my relational circles.

It is my intense desire that upon completion of this book, you, dear reader, will have laughed at some of the anecdotal stories herein or maybe allowed your eyes to "leak" in compassion and empathy toward those of whom I write in the following chapters. Lastly, I certainly hope that you will have thought about topics in ways you may never have done before. Too, it would be a great bonus if perchance you would, if not already doing so, be moved to consider the possibility of pursuing licensing your home and thus integrate into your family the children that need the essentials of your love and talents to help them negotiate the struggles of the trauma and tribulations to which they have been heinously subjected.

I fully realize that foster care and adoption are not for everyone. That said, I also know that there are abundant ways one can make a difference in the lives of our hurting youth that does not require the sacrifice of accommodating troubled kids in one's own home if that's just not feasible at this current juncture of one's life. Perhaps instead, mentoring a child in foster care would be more up one's alley by giving one or two hours a week in sharing various activities. Or maybe baby sitting for the foster/adoptive parents while they enjoy a much needed date night. Gift certificates for pizza, movies, prom dresses, high school yearbooks, etc. are always appreciated. Transportation can sometimes be a nightmarish issue so an offer to pick up groceries can be a godsend to those juggling the logistics of school, doctor appointments, therapy meetings, sports and the like. These are but a few sundry physical and emotional necessities for which one could assist with a caring, helping hand.

You are now a willing participant with me on a rollercoaster ride as I share with you stories from several different perspectives. Some of what you will read is from a human services worker view point while others will be from a foster/adoptive parent perspective. Still others will give a perspective of a national presenter who shares life from the trenches…knowledge and wisdom that I communicate with a passion to help others survive "vicarious trauma" which stems from being on the front lines with those dealing with deep battle scars of their own. Too, you will encounter a few of those I've influenced (and vice versa) who have given me permission to share with you glimpses into their world.

In any event, it is my wish this read will inspire and thus give hope to those whose hearts may have become somewhat hardened because of the woes of the world (been there, done that). I must add that as a man of faith, I do not apologize for sharing the Lord throughout this manuscript. God, in His infinite wisdom and everlasting mercy and love, has been my strong tower, my anchor and fortress through the fieriest of furnaces.

Some who partake of this writing will, of course, not share my faith and devotion to the Christian walk. I understand. Moreover, I pray that this fact will not be a hindrance to those of you embracing different worldviews. I believe there is so much herein that anyone of any belief system will gain some tidbit of encouragement from what I have to share. I purposely do not "shove my beliefs down throats" as that is not my plan or purpose. I recognize that everyone has a right to believe whatever they desire and thus live accordingly. I, nonetheless, still want to give all glory and honor to Jesus, my Risen King.

This book is a modest attempt to give readers an insight into the world of foster/adoptive care. Others before me might have more letters behind their names, more years of experience and even a greater ability to successfully connect with their families and clients. Nothing here is new except in the sense that it is an honest exploration of my own God-ordained journey with a myriad of both trials and delights.

Preface

While my passionate fire may not be comparably large, it is indeed genuine and there may be those who can light their candle at its flame.

So all that being said, it's time to grab a refreshing drink, sit back, put your feet up and relax as you embark with me on this excursion. And may I humbly ask that if you're a praying person, please feel free to lift some prayers to the Throne of Grace for the kids, the families and for those that serve them – and, of course, for me. I continue to covet any and all petitions concerning finishing the race well myself and that Jesus will be glorified in all that I do from now until the time He takes me Home.

M. Kim Combes, M.Ed.

Introduction

The following pages are reflective of the journey on which I invited you. The articles, essays and stories are compiled in the best sequential order I could arrange to replicate, in stepping-stone fashion, the progression I've made in said journey. Many of these articles were formerly published over several years in FOSTERING FAMILIES TODAY (FFT) magazine.

I had the extreme honor of meeting Richard Fischer, FFT's publisher, at a National Foster Parent Association conference where I boldly introduced myself and then courageously inquired as to whether there was any chance I could be an occasional guest writer for his new publication. After talking for quite some time, he heartily agreed that he and his editor at that time, Cynthia Peck, would take into consideration my request. They both gave "thumbs up" to my submissions and have since contributed several well-received articles to FFT. The following article written in 2001, is my debut venture into being a nationally published writer.

My name is MR. Kim Combes (male Kim means "leader or chief") and I would like to welcome you to issue two of this fine, fast-growing foster care magazine. I have the honor of trying to encourage and challenge all of you as you do your wonderful ministry...foster care and adoption of our society's most difficult children and teens. Seven years ago God called me to this. Here is my story.

It was on the first day of my practicum in a local children's shelter in February 1994 that several teens came walking in carrying Gideon Bibles handed them after school that day. Most of these young people were angry...shredding them, cussing God and mocking those who believe in Him. One male teen, Eddie, stated, "I don't even know if I believe in God, but if he exists, he is mean, cold, and cruel." As a believer, this struck my heart. I prayed for him, and for the others of similar mindset. I asked God to use me to help Eddie and his peers see Him differently.

I was not a novice in the human service arena. I had been a residence counselor in a children's home, an educational aide in a classroom for the behaviorally challenged, an Iowa Department of Human Service's social worker and, at that time, a foster care training specialist at Iowa State University in Ames, IA. Since college graduation in 1980, I had worked with myriad families and children with varied problems and familial dysfunctions. About the only job I had not yet done in this field was foster care.

Introduction

God does indeed work in mysterious ways. The more time I spent with this young man, Eddie, who was just out of residential placement, not able to return home, the more I felt the tug at my heart to provide a home for him. I contacted a licensing agency in March and by May 1st I was a licensed foster parent. Because Eddie's worker had attended some of my ISU trainings, I was able to sell myself to him as the best option for Eddie he presently had going for him. He concurred. On May 24, 1994 I became a parent to a young man who would be 16 in the next week. Little did I know (or I might not have ever become licensed) how much I was to learn about Eddie, myself, and God in the coming weeks and months.

It is my desire to encourage all readers (regardless of faith, beliefs and values) in their foster care journey. My faith is in Jesus, but I hope this won't be a hindrance to those who do not similarly believe. We are on this journey together regardless of where we gather our strength and endurance. The scars these youth sadly and yet courageously bring into our homes callous them to the love they need and ironically they push it away. Yet, we all commit to persevere in the midst of the struggle of parenting these kids with angry, armor-coated hearts that protect them from the ills of this world.

Eddie has been just one of many young men with whom I have had the honor of sharing my home. I have grown in my perspective of God and life as I have strived to answer the question "WWJD?" (What Would Jesus Do?) with these kids if they were in HIS home. I have failed and I have succeeded. It is with humbleness that I would like to share my walk with you, challenging each other to stand firm in our convictions... against all odds. Our future generation depends on it.

Safety Issues: Reflections of 9/11

As foster parents, safety is an important issue with the children we serve. Physical safety and/or emotional safety has typically been a key element missing in foster children's lives due to difficult circumstances, parental choices, or choices they themselves have made. Our first job when a child is placed in our home is to help him feel safe so that issues can be addressed and wounds can start to heal.

As citizens of the United States, our safety is something that we have taken for granted for years. That is, until Tuesday, Sept. 11. Now we, too, get a taste of fear, our own realization that what happens next may not be at all within our own control.

The breadth of the ramifications of this senseless terrorist attack will be far reaching into the future. None of us will ever be the same. Once secure within the confines of U.S. soil, our long-held façade is now toppled along with the twin towers in New York City. Where trust once dwelled fear now resides.

While the world is glued to their radios and televisions, questions arise in the minds of people everywhere. Who or what is the next target? Where can we go to be safe? Family and loved ones become the focus of our thoughts. Words of God, church and prayer are heard everywhere. Current events are suddenly bigger than what the human spirit alone can endure.

Conversations of spiritual nature are taking place from coast to coast, perhaps worldwide. Our foster teens came home from school incredulous of what was happening on the TVs they had been watching all day. Knowing that my wife and I are Christians, they asked questions regarding the Bible, God, "end times", etc. That night they watched a "Left Behind" movie from our video collection, again asking questions, challenging their own thinking (and ours) on a spiritual plane.

Do Diane and I have the answers? Do we know exactly how this horrific act fits into our belief system? Can we comfort their hearts and take away the fears that were not there prior to this day of carnage? NO, an emphatic NO. But to the best of our ability, we can pray for them, allow them to express their fears/beliefs and reassure them we will do all in our power to keep them safe in our home. This is the most that any of us as biological, step, adoptive and/or foster parents can do.

Safety Issues: Reflections of 9/11

We're at a time when all the problems we had before this infamous day seemed significant. Terrible Tuesday changed our perspective of many things about which we grumble daily. We've been more "enlightened" as to the brevity of life and all that is really important to us. We'll attempt, from here on out, to live more simply...a lesson we could have learned from impoverished, war-torn countries decades ago (funny how tragedy has to strike close to OUR home before certain truths start to sink in).

A recent New York Times Bestseller, THE PRAYER OF JABEZ by Bruce Wilkinson, comes to mind. This book espousing the power of a simple prayer from I Chronicles 4:9-10 has changed thousands of lives. Diane and me will continue to pray this prayer for our home and for our world throughout the coming days, whatever they hold:

"And Jabez called on God of Israel saying, 'Oh, that You would bless me indeed, and enlarge my territory, that Your hand would be with me, and that You would keep me from evil, that I might not cause pain!' So God granted him what he requested."

Kinship Care

My wife recently expressed to me her desire to swoop over Afghanistan rescuing orphaned young people, bringing to America as many as she could gather. Her heart has always been tender toward young children, especially babies and toddlers in horrendous situations such as is the plight of all Afghan children today.

Indeed, as foster/adoptive parents, our hearts hurt for the young people of this war-torn, or any war-torn, impoverished and disease-ridden nation. We would love to comfort fears and dry tears as great terror, loss and grief is expressed. And we do. Some of us have gone through adoption agencies such as Holt International. Others may have initiated private adoptions domestically while for yet others, such as Diane and me, the genesis of adoption was through fostering for a public agency. Some of us are strictly foster parents with no desire to adopt at all. In any event, our hearts are bent toward the unfortunate children who are experiencing their own terror and grief, even if they didn't come from the opposite end of the globe, but just from the other side of town.

As an ex- Iowa Department of Human Services worker and a former foster care specialist for a private agency, I have interacted with myriad foster children of all ages and foster/adoptive parents who do their best to love them. Some of those with whom I've worked have taken in as foster children their own nieces/nephews, brothers/sisters, grandchildren and even great-grandchildren. The mandates of PUBLIC LAW 96-272 dictate that the placing worker MUST first attempt to place a child in a relative home and document in the case permanency plan why that was not an option.

Kinship care, theoretically, is the best option when a child must leave the parental home. As a worker, I was not always privy to the "next of kin" when a court order was issued. And many times, for whatever reasons, the parents did not want their child going into a relative's care.

Moreover, I have heard workers and foster parents verbalize that "the nut doesn't fall very far from the tree" meaning if a parent is "messed up" then the whole family of origin must have major problems. In some cases, this may be true, but an overgeneralization of such is ALWAYS inappropriate. I have witnessed many devoted and committed aunts and uncles, grandparents and other family members give 150% to helping wayward youth get back on track. Whether or not the "new addition" will choose to do so is neither here nor there. These caregivers believed it was their

Kinship Care

"ministry" to do this. After all, family is family. They will rest assured they did the best they could to positively influence a young life.

I currently have a 15-year-old nephew in foster care less than an hour away. My brother, long separated from the mother of his child who was NOT given custody, did not want his son getting a "reward" for misbehavior by living with me, his favorite uncle. It has been 30-some months and Shawn is still in care, possibly looking at being adopted by his new family. Yes, it saddens all of us that events took this turn. However, I also believe that Shawn is being well cared for and doing much better with a greater chance of life success with the structure and guidance in his new environment (and his father reluctantly and sadly agrees). Would he choose to do as well in my home had Dad agreed to let him come here? Honestly…I don't know. Given the more street-wise, "delinquent" boys I have had in my home, Shawn might have gotten eaten alive. Ideally, adopted or not, the new family would allow all of us to keep contact. Currently, this is not happening and is explained away by the phrase "best interest of the child."

While my brother may have his issues, he loves his son. My family also loves him and has never been anything but nurturing and loving towards him. We are not monsters that will harm him, but generous and affectionate kin desiring only to help him be the best he can be. We miss him. Workers and others in the system need to be reminded that we all have "free will" and that even those raised in the best of families can choose a wrong road (and vice versa). Too, please withhold judgment and keep an open mind toward those of the same blood. While not perfect, these people can be the child's greatest asset…and the worker's.

Anything anyone does can be closely scrutinized and critiqued. Kinship care is no exception. Say what you will regarding the view that the nut doesn't fall far from the tree, it is still my belief that when possible, family members should always be considered as the first alternative to the biological home. Scripture tells us we are to care for widows and orphans. May God raise up more of us to do just that, whether the "orphans" are related or not. Heaven knows the whole world needs it.

Walk In A Manner Worthy

Post Adoption Dilemmas

He was desperate. "I really need help now," he almost begged. Franklin phoned me at his wit's end. What is a single adoptive dad of an angry 14-year-old to do when the adoption that was finalized last summer is on the brink of disruption and all pre-adoptive services have been curtailed?

Josh (not his real name) was becoming more and more demanding, allowing no peace in the house from early PM until way past bedtime. Josh would, even when planned ignoring was utilized, continue to yell, pound, stomp around and, in general, make life miserable for Dad and the pre-teen foster child living in their home. Talking only stirred up more of the "righteous indignation" about all the ills of his life. Dad, perplexed and discouraged, wanted out of the abyss of mayhem back to the semi-tranquility of his castle.

This is the plight of a majority of post-placement families desiring to give a child/teen a loving, nurturing family in which to grow and mature to adulthood. While Iowa has a great post-adoption program through the Iowa Foster/Adoptive Parents Association (IFAPA), it would seem that many families across our state and nation are left to fend for themselves after leaving the courtroom with the newest family member now bearing their name. To further illustrate, I share a scenario that graphically describes the background of myriad children placed in foster/adoptive homes. While specifics may differ, the ravages of the young human heart do not.

A foster family took two troubled brothers, less than age 10, into their home at the beginning of late winter. By early fall, manifested behaviors were manageable, Termination of Parental Rights (TPR) had occurred and adoption finalization was discussed as happening at the beginning of January. Shortly after Thanksgiving the youths' behaviors started to once again deteriorate. Involved adults could not determine what was happening. Did the boys NOT want to be adopted because of loyalty issues associated with the biological parents? Were they testing the new family's love and commitment toward them? Counseling revealed a part of their past that horrified the family.

Thanksgiving night tradition dictated the annual trimming of their Christmas tree. Underneath, presents with the boys' names attached were soon found. Because this was the boys' first holiday season with them, to show their love, the family lavished them with gifts. Unfortunately, this meant something TOTALLY different to the boys.

Post Adoption Dilemmas

Biological parents had bought gifts for the boys also...with strings attached. While in therapy, it was discovered that the boys were made to perform a sex act with the parents before receiving each "gift". The more presents, the more abuse that occurred. While looking at the number of presents surrounding their new family's tree, the boys' memories and emotions came flooding back from Christmases past.

This shocking story is not surprising to those who have fostered, adopted, or worked in the human service arena for any length of time. However, there are legislators and other influential people who appear uninformed as to the emotional baggage brought into homes with each new placement. I am aware of lawmakers who, surprisingly, still believe "love cures all" and once these kids are given permanency, normalcy returns to their lives and to the lives of their caregivers.

What will it take to capture the attention of our nation and states' governmental leaders as it relates to the ongoing trials in the homes of foster/adoptive parents who house society's most dysfunctional

Minor-aged members? Sadly, much education still needs to be done surrounding the issues of foster/adoptive care. We can agree with this truth and either sit back in stark resignation that "this is the way it will always be" or we can stand up, speak out and be heard.

I challenge all to write and/or call their local state representatives. Perhaps sending a copy of this article will open some ears deaf to this cause because of the big bucks potentially attached to a solution. Ironically, the very funds not spent on damaged children now will likely be spent on prisons and court costs (along with mental health dollars) after they reach the age of majority.

We can be the voice for those that don't yet have a legal voice. One letter or call to elected officials who make the laws, I've been told, represents approximately 100 constituents. There IS power in numbers. Complacency will not get the funding and services needed to keep foster/adoptive families intact. Nor will it keep families providing this tremendous service to children and teens that need them. Imagine the vast ramifications of all foster/adoptive parents nationwide simultaneously turning in their licensure - not that any of us would do that - but just imagine leaving the States to finance the alternative care of their now-homeless wards!

We can and DO make a difference. The time is now. Let's roll.

Walk In A Manner Worthy

Legislation Opportunities

Welcome to 2003. As I write this, Christmas is still two weeks away. For whatever reasons, I am having a hard time getting into the Christmas spirit this year. Perhaps it is because this year has seemed to zip by and it CAN'T POSSIBLY be Christmas yet. Yet another reason could be because of life's trials that try to rob me (and all of us) of the joy of the season. Too, it may be that I am looking into the upcoming year with great anticipation of all that it potentially holds, possibly skewing my vision and excitement in the short-term scheme of things.

We are all on the threshold of new experiences and adventures. We have before us a yet unblemished 365 days in which to write new chapters of our lives. How will we be different a year from now? What events will mold us into, hopefully, more mature and wiser individuals? How will our lives touch those in our circle? Will others be more blessed and have a richer, fuller life because we were in it? The questions, as well as the opportunities for good, are endless.

Allow me to share one event that I hope and pray will make an impact on many in the state of Iowa. This idea is not original and I want to thank people from the state of Nevada for sharing this at a National Foster Parent Association conference several years ago. The seed was planted in Orlando but took some time to come to fruition in Iowa. The following is a synopsis of their plan (as I remember it 5 years later).

Several years ago a group of dedicated and concerned foster parents from Nevada decided to give all lawmakers, at the beginning of the legislative session, a "throwaway" doll (hair pulled out, limbs missing, half-naked, etc). Each of these dolls represented the abused, neglected and "throw-away" children that Nevada foster/adoptive parents took into their homes. Each lawmaker was also given a case permanency plan to go with each doll. They were asked to give each of these dolls a "foster home" for the duration of the legislative session. They would agree to care for these little people, meeting all their needs, as if they were real. Long story short, before the end of the session, legislators found and reallocated approximately $70,000 towards helping the foster/adoptive care system in their state. How much money was in the original fund? ZIP. ZERO. NADA. The end result was well worth the energy and time expended.

Now, back to Iowa. On January 21, 2003, I am spearheading a "Storm the Hill" day. Even as I type, foster/adoptive parents are collecting dolls and preparing caseplans to give to the 150 lawmakers coming to Des Moines in January. Social workers

Legislation Opportunities

from both public and private agencies have been informed of this event. I will be sending editorials to several state newspapers. I will use all the media connections of which I am aware to cover this event. An elected official, also an avid child advocate, has agreed to sponsor a press conference for me at the Capital that day. I, and those helping me pull this together, want the general public to know how budget cuts are affecting foster/adoptive parents, and more importantly, the children we serve...the next generation.

Budget cuts last session were severe. Iowans do not anticipate it will be much better in 2003. However, we are guaranteed that nothing will change if we all sit at home, wringing our hands in discouragement, doing nothing. Perhaps we won't be able to stop the inevitable, but we can take a stand by letting elected officials know that their constituents are not pleased with the choices they are making concerning those for whom we are passionate. Time will tell what impact this will have for Iowa's children.

It might be too late in the session for you readers to get something going this legislative year. However, I share this to invite you, too, to take a stand. Rally your troops for NEXT year. Start campaigning now for the best interest of the children. If we don't do this, no one else will. Now is not the time for apathy. Now is not the time to think, "Well, it's a good idea, but somebody else can do this as I just don't have time". It won't happen unless we ALL do our part, working together for the common good.

I know we are all tired, and maybe even completely burned-out, caring for the difficult children we have in our homes. But still, my challenge is this: Start talking this up in your support groups. Get key people interested. Talk to your representatives. Write letters to the editor. I believe we CAN (and DO) make a difference.

I hope to have very encouraging news and more specifics of the day in the next issue. HAPPY NEW YEAR!!!!

Epilogue

It's been just over 17 years since STORM THE HILL. I wish I could look back at that experience as a success, but alas, it did not go as I anticipated. The idea in and of itself was good. Execution, however, was lacking in foresight on my part. Let me expound.

Walk In A Manner Worthy

In attendance were many foster/adoptive parents that were onboard with my plan to make a positive impact on our legislative body for the good of those placed in our homes. However, I failed to address in my planning the negative issues that would be brought to the table by those who had a bone to pick with those steering the system. Instead of coming to our leaders in a gracious soft-spoken manner, there were a handful that brought their agenda of complaints and gripes and, for a lack of better term, "vomited" all their venom on these unsuspecting elected officials we were supposed to woo, not decapitate. Needless to say, I took plenty of heat for the outcome of this fiasco event.

Should anyone desire to attempt such an occasion after reading of my experience, I would first adamantly suggest that there would be prior legislative training sessions on the proper etiquette of making friends and influencing people – that and perhaps hand-picking a dozen or so individuals trustworthy of such an undertaking, both of which would greatly enhance the atmosphere of such a powerful commission. Nuff said bout that.

Foster/Adoptive Care Training

It was 15 years ago this Spring that I entered into the foster care system on the other side. I had been an Iowa Department of Human Services (DHS) Social Worker II for five years prior to deciding to get myself licensed to take in a 15 year old young man whom I met doing my Master's Degree internship at a local children's shelter in Ames. Little did I know then how much Eddie would change the course of my life a decade and a half later.

I was not new to the human service arena prior to having Eddie become a member of my single parent household. I had previously been employed as a youth worker in a residential treatment center, an educational aide in a classroom for behaviorally challenged high school students as well as a DHS worker where I also had my share of challenging youth and families. But in all honesty, these experiences did not fully prepare me for what lay ahead.

I was employed by Iowa State University's Child Welfare Research and Training Program from 1989-1994 where I developed and delivered trainings to Iowa DHS Social Workers and, on occasion, foster/adoptive parents. Most of this training was geared toward rules and regulations guiding the Iowa foster care/juvenile court system. Upon leaving ISU I freelanced as a national presenter, developing seminars to better equip foster/adoptive parents in dealing with the ongoing challenging behaviors of their charges. I transitioned from "book training" to "trench training" within a short amount of time.

While fostering four teen boys in my home, I also worked for three years as a full time private agency in-home worker, providing services to foster/adoptive parents who were struggling, just as I now was, with how to best deal with a gamut of behaviors manifested in our households. This was challenging for me at best as I had no real break from the stress caused by the chaos troubled youth brought into my life, both at work and at home.

I have always enjoyed learning and thus I signed myself up for as many parenting and social work courses as I could, knowing that I needed as much help as I could get, both personally and professionally. Historically I get excited about gaining a new concept, a new skill, a new perspective which would, theoretically anyway, make my life easier while also engaging my children/clients in rethinking some dysfunctional thought patterns leading to destructive, antisocial outcomes. I soon learned, much to my chagrin, that "theory" had some shortcomings.

Walk In A Manner Worthy

I naively believed I was a pretty patient person prior to bringing rambunctious teen boys into my up-until-now quiet dwelling place. While I did the best I could with the knowledge gained through schooling, my patience level was sorely tested as my young men exuded their less-than-acceptable behaviors in ways that definitely pushed my buttons. I soon came to realize that the façade of control I assumed I had was now crumbling rapidly. Reality was this: the only thing I had control of was how I responded to the things I didn't have control of. The training I experienced up to this point now seemed ineffective. Much more was obviously needed. I had been trying so hard to mold and shape my guys into who I believed they should become that I was blinded to the work I needed to do in myself to become the mentor they needed to mold and shape themselves. This realization was a turning point in my life. I will return to this point shortly.

Over the years I have attended myriad training seminars ranging in length from 3 hours to 5 days. Too, I have experienced trainers who made 3 hour trainings seem like 5 days and vice versa. Regardless of how great the material might be, if my style of learning is not incorporated into the presentation format, I will zone out.

My attendance at seminars the last 20 years has been two-fold. My first priority is to gain new information that I can hopefully use in practical everyday life and perhaps integrate into my own presentations. The second is to watch and learn new presentation techniques...either what to emulate in my own seminars or make a mental note of what never to do as a presenter in a training situation.

Heather Craig-Oldsen is my first and most favorite mentor in the training field. She has been instrumental in helping me develop my own training style, cheering me on when I might have otherwise chosen to wave the white flag of surrender while fostering and training. Although she has not been a foster/adoptive parent, she has been in the social work trenches both personally and professionally thus bringing with her much to share with those of us who are. Her style and presentation techniques are superb. Her humor and warmth draw out various personalities in her audiences. She presents herself very professionally, yet is a very down to earth individual who exudes caring and concern while presenting. I share this because she has made such a huge impact on me...as well as many others that have attended her seminars. She, to me, is the ideal for presenter standards.

As a professional presenter, I strive to instruct in a way that incorporates those who learn visually, audibly, and kinesthetically (hands on), as Heather has taught me. I use humor and real-life stories from my own experience. I share with my audiences my successes and many of my failures as I attempted to parent challenging children. If my evaluations are any indication, the most powerful training tool I have is "trench" material, which I have gained from the trials and tribulations of foster and adoptive care, coupled with my social work experiences. It makes sense to me that participants find more credible those that have lived the experience contrasted to those that have learned it from formal education. There is a time and place for the formality of research in training; however, I have found that those of us in the foxholes of life seem to find the camaraderie of shared experiences more powerful in the learning process.

That all said, I need to return to the previous point made about needing to change myself to influence others. I've gleaned from experience that the most effective training is not learning how to manage others, but how to control oneself for the sake of others. Eddie gave me ample opportunity to practice this. My five adopted children are reaping the rewards of what I have learned from Eddie and those that followed.

While nowhere near perfect, I have changed my thinking greatly about how I now respond to the parenting challenges presented in our home. Diane and I have worked diligently to change how WE respond rather than pour wasted energy into changing our kids. We are discovering that our kids are positively changing as we morph from our more angry responses to responding with calm acceptance of our children, while pointing out the error of their ways. Another influential person in the training field taught me that our children "will not heal nor attach to angry caregivers."

Trauma freezes the brain and our kids get stuck in ODD (Oppositional Defiant Disorder) mode when feeling threatened, intimidated and/or unsafe whether the trigger is real or imagined. Parental anger, which our kids are great at provoking, hinders our kids from the potential growth they could make in a calmer, more nurturing environment. I am disappointed in myself as to how many times I have responded in less-than-calm ways to the behaviors we observe in our home daily. Nonetheless, Diane and I are improving in how we manage ourselves for the sake of the kids.

In conclusion, all the training in the world will be fruitless if we as parents fail to recognize the paramount importance of changing ourselves before we attempt to change the behaviors in our kids. I cannot in good conscience teach something that I do not believe in passionately and I have seen firsthand the difference in our chil-

Walk In A Manner Worthy

dren in the last few years as Diane and I focus on us, rather than the misbehaviors of our awesome kids. We still have a long way to go but, by God's grace, we are getting there. I am certain that if I can do this, it is indeed possible for others to accomplish this also. My prayers are with you.

Just 1 Person by Travis Lloyd

This next article (Just 1 Person by Travis Lloyd) is yet another from FOSTERING FAMILIES TODAY magazine. However, I am not the author. I asked permission of Travis Lloyd to use this as it resonated with me and was impacted by this writing. Travis, interestingly, was a young man that had connections to one of my former teen foster sons, James, whom you will meet further on in this book. I did not have the pleasure of meeting Travis back then, however, even though he had been to my home.

I met Travis at one of our state trauma-informed-care meetings in Des Moines several years ago. I had heard of Travis prior to meeting him as he was making a difference statewide in the work he was doing in the mental health field. He is an "ashes to beauty" guy, utilizing lessons of his own dysfunctional background to make a difference in supporting those struggling in similar ways as he had. Travis now has a huge following because of open doors that led him into international presenting - that, and having a book he penned a few years ago...a book I was asked to endorse, which I was honored to do.

You may learn more about Mr. Lloyd at the conclusion of this article. Thanks, Travis, for all you do.

Walk In A Manner Worthy

Just 1 Person by Travis Lloyd

The phrase "Just 1 Person" is a phrase that I have found to be powerful and effective for creating an emotional connection to the desire (and need) for a change of heart, perspective, and eventually a systemic change in the systems we navigate as parents, advocates, professionals, and overall people who simply take the time to care.

I have found this phrase especially impactful when speaking to both public and private child-serving groups or organizations. Considering child-serving organizations comprise approximately 75% of the presentations I do across the country, it is fitting that one of my most requested keynote presentations holds the title Just 1 Person.

As I was seeking inspiration for this article I wanted to veer from simply regurgitating the same material that I use on stage so I did some online research to identify what "Just 1 Person" means to Google.

I was expecting to find some scientific research and maybe some statistics to reference, but what I found was quite the opposite. What I found did not complicate things or require a spreadsheet of stats and facts. It was as simple as the original intent of the stories I share on stage and that is the very concrete idea of connecting to someone's heart, meeting them where they are, and being 100% mentally and emotionally present allowing us to have the best possible impact on those around us. Considering this bit of affirmation, I decided to utilize my research not to replace the stories I already share, but rather to enhance and reinforce them.

The first article I came across when googling "Just 1 Person" was one that shared the story of a puppeteer, artist, screen writer, and producer named Jim Henson. You might better recognize him as the man behind Bert and Ernie from Sesame Street.

This story highlighted his unfortunate passing and the celebration of life that followed in place of a standard funeral service. Per Jim's documented request, his celebration of life was filled with fun, music, and positivity. When reviewing the event videos on YouTube and learning about this powerful individual I watched a performance of a song titled "Just One Person" that this article states "originated as a Muppet classic back when little Robin the Frog needed to be uplifted." This was undoubtedly chosen to highlight the vast impact that Henson individually had not just on those around him, but on American culture and societies across the world.

Just 1 Person by Travis Lloyd

It is easy to view someone with such a large presence as having accomplishments that are unattainable by the average citizen. Such a viewpoint makes it easy for us to remain complacent in our life, relationships, and perceived level of success in each. However, the simplicity of the song Just One Person as it is utilized to portray the life-long efforts of this one shining individual allows us to apply that same principle to our lives, relationships, and systems that we navigate every day. In order to do so we must be willing to view our daily interactions as just as impactful as Henson's characters Bert and Ernie.

Yes, Bert and Ernie were able to touch millions of individuals and, in turn, create a positive societal influence. But each opportunity we have to interact with a friend, family member, colleague, or young person in our lives is just as impactful. I would challenge you to see it as even more impactful than a television show spreading across nations. Human to human interaction has a stronger impact than any media can have, but we must choose to see the value in it. We must choose to recognize how we, as Just 1 Person each, can shape the minds, views, and perceptions of those around us; especially the most influential traumatized young people.

I recently met with a friend of mine who is now the director of communications and fundraising for a large health care organization. He informed me that the perception that the community has of the organization is that their facilities only exist to serve the "poor" populations as "free clinics" when that is not the case. A large part of this negative perception within the community is due to their branding not being adequate. They don't have up to date signage or even courtesy signs that gently remind patients to cover their mouth when they cough in the waiting room.

A physician took things into her own hands and printed signs out of word documents to solve some of these problems that were consistently arising in her clinic. The signs were unprofessional and rather unfriendly in the wording for such reminders. Instead of being a nicely printed professional sign it was a standard piece of printer paper reading "REMINDER: COVER YOUR MOUTH WHEN YOU COUGH." This did not go over well with administration and one of the initial concerns was a reaction to the fact that a physician who is paid $130 per hour to treat patients actually spent some of her time creating paper signs.

I saw this as an opportunity to apply the basic principles of Trauma Informed Care Practices (TICP) to the health care/corporate environment. It was easy to identify that this situation was very similar to a parent and child situation.

Walk In A Manner Worthy

If a young child was hungry and went to the kitchen to cook an egg, but then dropped the egg the parent could easily be angered and respond with consequences for making a mess. But a more understanding approach might be to ask the child if they are hungry and then help them learn how to better cook an egg without making a mess.

In the above situation, the parent is the health care organization's administration and the child is the physician. Instead of being angered of the potential financial concerns, the administration could instead assign the job of creating signage to an employee who is more fit for that specific task. That employee could then work in collaboration with the physician to provide her clinic with the signage they are lacking. It could then be done in a more effective and acceptable manner.

Just like the administration and the parent, we get to choose how we respond in similar moments of crisis. Regardless of a situation's level of significance we must approach each situation with an open heart and a desire to understand the reasoning behind behaviors. It is all too easy to react to things negatively and it takes a conscious effort to approach individuals in a way that offers reassurance and guidance rather than judgement and shaming. Remember, we may not remember the name of a person, but we will always remember the way they made us feel. This is the biochemistry behind first impressions and every moment of crisis presents a new opportunity for an impression to be imprinted in another's mind.

I can share from personal experience the power of impressions, both positive and negative, and how two specific incidences during my childhood shaped my memory of two individuals and my own perception of myself as a youth.

The first experience was a memory of my probation officer when I was 13. After completing my 100 hours of community service I felt very proud of my accomplishments and was excited to go to the final visit with my probation officer. My aunt drove me to the appointment where my probation officer presented with her standard flat mood, signed the release papers, and informed my aunt as we were leaving, "We'll probably see you again in a couple of years. They usually come back." How bitter! I don't remember her name, but when I was down and out as a teen I sometimes thought of that moment and it made it okay to do wrong because she had helped shape who I was expected to be and I was expected to be bad.

The second experience was that of my eighth grade language arts teacher. On the final day of school I was excited to go out in the sun and be free for the summer! I

Just 1 Person by Travis Lloyd

was hastily walking the halls and almost reached the main exit when I felt a hand on my shoulder. Mrs. Ross stood about my height and I would guess she was about 90 pounds dripping wet. I honestly thought that I was going to be in trouble and I remember thinking to myself, "How could they suspend me on the last day of school when I'm already leaving the building?!

But that worry quickly dissipated when Mrs. Ross spoke in a calm voice as she informed me that she and the science teacher Mr. Fedler felt that they wanted me to know something. She continued to inform me that together they felt that I had been the most improved through the year and that she was proud of me and that she felt I would do really well in high school.

In that moment, Mrs. Ross became Just 1 Person to make a positive difference and reminded me of the greatness I could not see in myself. That reminder helped me push through some of the worst moments of my life that were yet to come as a youth wandering aimlessly in pursuit of finding, or creating, my own identity.

I encourage you to be the Jim Henson and Mrs. Ross in someone else's life. Whether large moments or small moments there are always opportunities to make an impression. Please make an impression that will allow someone to feel good and remember your name 20 years later. Maybe you'll be the one they write about in their next article. (Fostering FAMILIES TODAY magazine May/June 2014 pp 36-38)

Travis Lloyd is an international motivational speaker and consultant primarily serving organizations and events that focus on creating systemic change within child welfare, juvenile justice, and mental health services. He is the President of the national non-profit Foster Care Alumni of America and has long been an advocate for at-risk populations. In 2014 he authored the book Overcoming Emotional Trauma: Life Beyond Survival Mode with contributions from the late Dr. Gregory Keck which highlights Mr. Lloyd's personal stories and advice for overcoming traumatic experiences and has been utilized in clinical practices and educational settings across the U.S. and abroad. He is passionate about home renovation projects, hip-hop music, and sunshine! Join Travis on Twitter: @TravisLloyd.

Walk In A Manner Worthy

Educating Foster And Adoptive Parents
(and those with whom they work)

I have been a foster parent since May 1994 when I took into my home (and heart) a young man whom I met while doing my Master's degree practicum at Rosedale Shelter in Ames, IA. I had been in the human service profession since 1980 when I got hired directly out of college as a residence counselor at a residential facility also in Ames. I have, too, tried my hand at the Iowa Department of Human Services where I delivered services to families in Story County Iowa. My path thus crossed with many foster and adoptive parents in the 14 years I was employed in this arena leading up to taking my first placement.

As a "wet behind the ears" young social worker with a passion to help children and families I realized in retrospect that I was pretty clueless as to what I was doing, flying by the seat of my pants in many situations. It was my interaction with wonderful devoted foster and adoptive families that kept me going when it would have been easy to throw in the towel with some of my clients who seemingly had no desire to change, thus staying in the same rut that subsequently got me into their lives initially.

As I reflect, I have to acknowledge that much of my own "professional training" came from those foster/adoptive parents who had been working with young people for years. Thankfully, there were also colleagues that were willing to enlighten me when I had no idea what to do next.

Times have greatly changed since my first foray into the human services field over a quarter century ago. The types of children being court-ordered into the facility in which I worked are today being put into brand, spanking new licensed foster family homes. Youth needing out of home placements today are frequently dual-diagnosed, many of them having more letters in the diagnosis than has alphabet soup. Furthermore, state coffers are in dire straits which further hinder agencies from placing these children in the structured environment that would best meet their varied needs. Hence, workers are forced to peruse the listing of current foster families with open beds. Sadly, good "matching" as well as pre-placement visits sometimes, if not always, go out the window.

The ramifications of this are far reaching... more disrupted placements, more trauma needing healed (for families and for the displaced children), prolonged stints in foster care, more worker dissatisfaction and subsequent turnover and fewer foster/adoptive families because of the negativity that gets around by "word of mouth."

Educating Foster and Adoptive Parents
(and Those With Whom They Work)

People with hearts for this much needed (and maligned) ministry seem to be getting fewer and fewer on a national level.

Depressed yet??? While this trend does not a pretty picture make, there are still those of us who have hope that we can indeed make a difference in the lives of hurting children and teens. But it will take a concerted effort from all involved in the child welfare system.

Let's revisit the status of those newly licensed foster parents, yet wearing the rose-colored glasses we have all worn early in our journey into the foster care system. Training and education beyond a shadow of doubt is key to the success of our crumbling structure. The next generation does indeed need us to place value on them, prioritizing governmental, if not grassroots efforts, to get funding for educating all parents on how to deal with the crises of our children and teens.

Days gone by would dictate a "good old fashioned whipping" behind the woodshed to take care of rebellious and strong-willed youth attitudes. Today, incidents of abuse allegations and findings are rising yearly. Children need much more than a switch across the rump to turn things around. Foster/adoptive parents, in particular, are dealing with children with much trauma in their lives. Loss and grief issues are running rampant in a society that refuses to honor our "throw away" kids. Parents place mood altering substances, passionate sex partners, jobs, etc. over the care and nurturing of the children they bring into the world. New techniques are needed to raise emotionally healthy children and future adults.

Being a foster/adoptive parent and a trainer, I have learned that I still have much to learn as to how to be the best I can be to help my kids negotiate adolescence and come out on the bright side of adulthood. However, in many years of traveling nationally I have discovered that there are many wonderful people with a plethora of knowledge they are passionate about sharing with seekers such as me. Given this, I am challenging readers to glean from others' wisdom concepts that we cannot possibly learn on our own (there just isn't time to make all the mistakes that would reap the harvest bringing us to "sage" status). Therefore, let's learn from what many can teach us from their parenting blunders (of which I've made many).

It has been my extreme privilege to have learned from many top-notch individuals who have been through the gauntlet, yet still undauntedly champion the cause of foster care and adoption. I know from my travels that every state in the U.S. has many talented people willing to share their experiences with those of us hungry to study the art of parenting. Most states have foster care/adoption associations that offer annual conferences where parents can gain state mandated training hours for licensure. There is available to all of us (foster/adoptive parents, social workers, therapists, teachers, day care providers, etc.) much innovative and cutting-edge information needed for us to survive in the trenches as we struggle with how to best deal with various behaviors confronting us daily. We NEED training, good training for, as the saying goes, "If you always do what you've always done, you'll always get what you've always gotten." New thought provoking ideas and concepts gleaned from presentations can literally change our lives, and thus the lives of those we serve.

There is another old adage that states: "Give a man a fish, feed him for a day. Teach a man to fish, feed him for a lifetime." This may be a stretch to some, but for me, it means that as we learn about parenting from those who have "been there, done that", we, too, have the tools we need daily to help our children (at least invite them) to make good choices leading to stability and a happy life. We limit ourselves greatly, and thus our children, when we as professionals (yes, foster parents are PROFESSIONALS) continue to try the one or two techniques our parents used on us rather than take advantage of the aforementioned knowledge available throughout the U.S.

For those foster/adoptive parents and professionals who still sport the rose-colored glasses, take note. They will break and you will need more than love to help you help the children placed in your devoted care. When this happens, utilize, too, the Web for much information on parenting. Connect with group list-serves that bring many people together to share common problems, to ask questions, seek and give encouragement or just share some humor in the midst of a trying day.

I cannot emphasize enough the paramount importance of expanding our knowledge base either through reading, DVD trainings, or via live conferences. Our kids and clients need us to be at our best. That will happen only when we value the learning process and are willing to devote both time and money to this end. Young lives depend upon it.

What kids need to get "past the past"

Hurt. Hopeless. Helpless. Fearful. Distrustful. Confused. ANGRY!!!! These are but a few of the adjectives describing a gamut of emotions youth in foster care bring into our lives. This emotional baggage can be overwhelming to the child and to all who work with these youth, regardless of the years of experience under their belts.

I've been in the human service arena in one capacity or another for over a quarter century. The driving force behind why any of us in this field do what we do is, or should be, the "best interest of the child". The million-dollar question, however, is "how do we, as human service professionals, manifest 'best interest' in our jobs given the ton of baggage mentioned above?"

Abraham Maslow, one of many psychotherapists who has studied human nature, came to the conclusion that there is a "hierarchy" of needs for all of us. He believes that more basic needs must be met before higher-level motives become active.

According to Maslow's Hierarchy principle, the basic biological needs, such as food, water, touch, etc. must be met before anyone can proceed to the next level. The second tier of needs is that of safety. The third, which will not be fulfilled until the safety needs are met, is that of love and belonging. In order to go to the fourth level of needs, self-esteem, one has to believe that one is loved and has a sense of belonging. The last level, self-actualization - the culmination of all that we are, will not reach full potential until the former four levels of need have been met.

Many have had "failure to thrive" children in their care or on their caseload. This diagnosis is given to children who have not had their needs met on the very basic level. These children are not going to feel safe until they believe they will have food and other necessities when they need it (hoarding is a sign that children do not yet trust their basic needs will be met, regardless of long-term proof contrary to their belief system). Kids who have been physically or sexually abused will have a hard time moving toward loving/belonging as they anticipate people will hurt them, thus they push others away by their behaviors so as not to get close. Should these children and teens reach the loving/belonging stage (many do this by joining "gangs" as they don't believe they fit in anywhere else), self-esteem will be difficult to attain. But as it is with all of us, unless we see ourselves in a positive framework, becoming "all that we can be" is next to impossible, even by joining the army.

Walk In A Manner Worthy

In addition to all my human service experience, I started fostering teenage boys 14 years ago this spring as a single foster dad. Diane joined me in this ministry nine years ago, bringing with her an 11-year-old daughter. Six months later we fostered a 10-½ month old boy who a year later became our legal adopted son. We have learned much together in this joint venture. It was not without pain and many tears, but we are seeing the rewards of the emotional energy we have invested in those that have been a part of our family. Too, our former teens, now adults, are enlightening us as to what they needed and wanted from us when they were living in our home.

So, what do we as caretakers do to help our charges get "past their past"? The obvious answer is to help each child at the level of needs he/she is at when they come into our home. This process builds the trust cycle, albeit very slow in coming. But is there more?

Several years ago at the National Foster Parent Association conference in Des Moines, I facilitated a panel discussion consisting of several former and one current foster teen. One panelist was nearing her 50s, if memory serves. These brave souls volunteered to make themselves vulnerable to pretty much any questions asked by the audience. While the inquiries varied, to me the overall answer of what best helped them work towards successful adulthood was this: genuine caring of a concerned individual(s) who was willing to stick with them through thick and thin as they negotiated the pitfalls of having to deal with the emotions/behaviors resulting from life's blows and the deep woundedness of their hearts and souls.

Hmmm, pretty simple task, huh? Easier said than done. These kids are experts at pushing buttons and thus pushing us away. Day in and day out, some of the behaviors families endure could push even Job over the top.

Recently I ran into two former clients, one whom I supervised in foster care a decade ago, the other whom I served through Family Centered Services back in 1985. Both recognized me but it took several seconds for me to recognize them, as I had not seen them since they were adolescents. Both reported the impact I'd had during a tumultuous time in their lives. The former foster child, when asked, reported to me that without his foster parents, he would probably be in prison today. He went on to say that it was because he "felt safe", was listened to, and was accepted as part of this family that he reached a turning point in his life. This youth had been sexually abused and was also a perpetrator in his teen years. He would urinate in his bedroom, lie, steal, masturbate in public and do anything to gain negative attention.

What Kids Need to Get "Past the Past"

I know there are myriad success stories amongst the readership of this magazine (FFT). I, alone, have enough stories of personal experience, coupled with stories others have related to me as I've traveled the U.S., to fill a book.

What was the secret of helping my charges through the tumultuous issues of their past? I believe it is a combination of many things. First, as mentioned, meeting the basic physical needs and the need for safety. Next, by doing the best I could, by the grace of God, I attempted to give my teen boys and those on my caseload unconditional positive regard. I failed on many occasions. I reached my boiling point more often than I care to admit. However, through it all, my prayers, my desire to be genuine, my stick-to-itiveness all paid off. Thousands of readers can relate, of this I am confident.

There is no magic elixir or wand that one can wave over another to "cure" the pain of the past. The internal scars of our children go deep. I would not continue to stay in this field if I did not believe that people could change. I have seen it. I, too, am a product of the influence of those that believed in me as I was growing up. No, I was not in foster care, but I struggled with self-esteem and depression. I had suicidal thoughts as an adolescent, feeling alone in an unsafe world. But through it all, I had the love of my family and close friends that kept me going…the ways we all do with the youth we serve.

I want to encourage all those in the human service field to continue striving, even in the face of being rejected by those whom we want to serve. Success is not measured by how our society views it. Success is not necessarily getting a good job, getting married and having 2.5 kids. For some of our kids, it's staying out of jail and/or prison. For others, it is being able to control one's anger in stressful situations or having a place to go for Christmas. One teen reported that he was thankful for having a family or significant adult that would house his high school yearbooks for him; having a place he viewed as safe and loving when the world became overwhelmingly frightening.

Perhaps we will never hear the youth thank us for what we've done as some have done for me. But don't for a second believe that the work and energy exerted to serve the children we have on our caseloads or in our homes is for naught. Many may not have this same value system, but for me, there is a verse in the Bible that I think of EVERY DAY, giving me the strength to continue in the ministry that Diane and I share in our home: *"Therefore brethren, stand firm. Let nothing move you. Always*

Walk In A Manner Worthy

give yourself fully to the work of the Lord for you know that your labor in the Lord is not in vain!" (I Corinthians 15:58).

Regardless of religious or personal convictions that drive one to passionately work with our next generation, reality is: YOU DO MAKE A DIFFERENCE. As a co-laborer in this field, on both ends of the human service continuum, I applaud all who sacrifice sleep, possessions, personal comfort, goals, time and energy for the sake of the children that need the secure relationship of one caring and nurturing individual in their lives.

I want to conclude with this adage, one that I have hanging on my office wall, to remind all of the significance and the paramount importance of what we do:

> "A hundred years from now it will not matter what my bank account was, the sort of house I lived in, or the kind of car I drove—but the world may be different because I was important in the life of a child." -Forest Witcraft

A letter written to my friend, Bryan Post

I want to share a story that happened last Wed night, just one day after we were with you. Jose, our 16 year old, has been a sore spot for us for over a year now with rollercoaster rides of his good vs not so hot choice-making while living here.

Last week, Diane found two pages of very emotional journaling that Jose wrote, pouring out his pain of losing Mom in death to other feelings he has been experiencing. One line in these pages was "F*** God, f*** friends, f*** family, I just want out of here". He went on to write that he cries himself to sleep, wants to run away, questioning whether anyone really understands him. It hurt my heart to read his journaling. When I tried to pursue him about this stuff (he doesn't know we saw his writing) he denied feeling any pain regarding his mom (whose funeral was two years ago Saturday). I tried my best to invite him to share his heart with me.

Jose got out of school early on Wednesday for teacher in-service day. Nine hours later, I discovered from his older brother, that he had broken about ten rules of our home while out with friends all day (not telling us where he was, being where he would not have had permission to be, etc). I thought about your conference and how you guys would handle that. When he got home after youth group that same night (an hour late), I was sitting on the porch swing - waiting. I asked him to have a seat on the stairs in front of me. I told him I was feeling hurt, helpless, hopeless and powerless to help him to negotiate life. I apologized for not being the father he needed to feel safe enough to let me into his world. I verbalized more specifically my fears, told him how much I loved him and how I would love to have a magic wand to take away his pain. Jose, who RARELY sheds tears, was wiping tears as we spoke. He knew, by the way, that I would be talking with him as his friend, Blake, told him I talked to him at youth group about the choices both he and Jose had made earlier in the day thus Jose was probably fearful of coming home choosing, then, to return late. After about 15-20 minutes, I asked Jose if I could move from the swing to the steps to sit by him. He said yes, that was okay. I also told him that given the degree of compassion I felt for him right then, I would probably start crying as soon as I changed spots.

Sure enough, I did. I grabbed his arm and put my head into his shoulder and cried. He grabbed me and held me close, shedding tears also. I started praying out loud, asking God to help me be a better dad to Jose, asking God to let Jose know how much He loved him, etc. When I stopped, the miracle happened. Jose started

Walk In A Manner Worthy

praying and crying, asking God to forgive him. Asking God to help him be the leader Dad said he could be. Asking God to help him quit making bad choices to be who He wanted him to be. This of course triggered more tears in me...tears of complete joy. Jose has refused to pray with me for over a year. He was now doing it on his own.

We just sat next to each other, crying and holding each other. Again, I apologized for not being the dad he needed and for the times I responded to him in hurtful ways out of my own fear. I asked him to forgive me. He looked at me and said "You are the dad that I need." He stood up, pulled me up by my hands and hugged me tightly, saying THANK YOU. We then went to bed...hope-filled. The next night, we prayed again. I thanked him for the awesome memory of the night before.

Yesterday at church a lady asked me what was different about Jose because he looked different...less angry. I told her. Too, Jose took communion for the first time in over a year. I had in the past advised him not to take communion if he truly was not believing in God, if he didn't want to forgive or be forgiven. So he chose not to partake which was congruent with his beliefs (for which I gave him kudos). He had never taken communion just because everyone else did.

Later that night I led my Young Men's Group at church. Around a roaring fire to ward off the early autumn chill, I taught a lesson about forgiveness and God's love and mercy us. I challenged them to forgive those who have hurt them and to ask forgiveness from those they know they have hurt. As Jose and I were walking into the building after talking all this time around a bonfire, he stopped me, looked straight into my eyes and said "Dad, will you please forgive me for all the times I hurt you and Mom?" WAIT A MINUTE...what?!!!? Is this my son? What a miracle.. AGAIN. He even prayed with the group before I dismissed the formal time of teaching that I had been doing.

Long story short, I am not sure I would have responded as I did had I not just come from a great day with you. An "old school" response would have escalated his fears, pushed him away, made a bigger chasm between the two of us; subsequently, he would NEVER have cried and asked God to forgive him. THANK YOU for your role modeling, showing me how to better love our troubled, pained kids.

Parenting With Pizazz

Many of us remember Redd Foxx in the 1970's sitcom Sanford and Son. He and his son co-owned a junk yard and interacted with various comedic individuals on a weekly basis. Fred Sanford had a trademark gesture for which he was well noted when excited. He would look to the heavens exclaiming "It's the big one, Elizabeth" to his deceased wife as he held his hand over his chest feigning near death by heart attack. Bystanders rolled their eyes as they witnessed this hyperbolic response to whatever it was Fred was reacting to in this overly melodramatic way.

A while back I attended a workshop called "Teenage Brains: Engines Without Drivers," Gloria and Lee Daniels presented research showing that as children hit puberty and negotiate adolescence, their brains "morph" much as brains do in the first five years of life. The turbulence of hormone surges, changing bodies, roller-coaster relationships and the angst that is associated with young adulthood makes parenting these aliens in our home challenging at best. Since parenting is sometimes a "crapshoot" we must have a full toolbox of ideas as to how to successfully negotiate teen life with our young charges. What works one day with our children may not work the next. So where do we start?

I believe children and teens respond to what they get the most response from. For example, sadly, my own children sometimes see the more frustrated side of my parenting rather than the delight I have in them when they are making good choices. If we continue to show more intense emotion for the negative choices our teens make, then show little or no emotion for good choices, we likely will get the behaviors that manifest our more emotional side. Thus, we need to learn to 'parent with pizzazz', doing the Fred Sanford imitation when good choices are made.

We can stop making a Federal case about chores not being done on time, grades being less than what we expect or attitudes being defiant. Rather, we can learn to exaggerate our responses to positive behaviors such as bringing home a good test score, starting a chore without being reminded, being nice to their brother, etc. Imagine our teens' response if we would grab our chest and celebrate loudly the fact that they were up on time without our awakening them, cleaned up a mess without prompting and showed initiative by starting homework before their designated time period for doing so. Yes, they may initially think we've finally "lost it", but done without sarcasm, with a playful smile and a hug or high five afterwards, these responses may motivate them to do more behaviors that have us responding as the fools they sometimes think we are. Moreover, it will give them something to razz us about in the presence of their kids someday like "Hey Junior, you should have seen how funny Grandpa looked back when I was a kid when he'd grab his heart like he was having a heart attack."

Teens are really no different than we adults when it comes to wanting respect and dignity from significant others. As difficult as it might seem sometimes, we need to remember that we wouldn't treat our boss, our friends, co-workers or members of the community the way we sometimes react to our children when they fail to meet our expectations. We need to come up with ways to discipline (lead, guide, teach, correct) our teens in ways that they feel respected...gently yet firmly.

Dr's. Gary Chapman and Ross Campbell co-authored "The Five Love Languages of Children" while Dr. Chapman alone wrote "The Five Love Languages of Teens." The premise of these books is that our children need all five love languages incorporated into their lives, but are hardwired for a primary love language...one that "fills their love tank". The authors believe it's not a question of "do we love our children, but do our children feel loved?"

The five love languages include physical touch, words of affirmation, quality time, gifts and acts of service. Many people give the same love language they desire to receive. For example, a parent who enjoys physical touch and close proximity to significant others will show their love by touching and being close. Teens, however, may try to avoid touch with parents; the parent subsequently feels rejected and the teen's own love language is overlooked. The teen may greatly desire quality time with a parent while the parent is blissfully ignorant of this yearning while the teen may manifest anything but that longing. Consequently the teen does not feel loved even while touchy-feely parents are trying diligently to convey their affection by hugging, high fives, hair mussing, etc.

Many young people respond well to words of affirmation..praise for good choices, high marks at school, random acts of kindness and the like. Some youth enjoy gifts... little tokens given them for the aforementioned choices (doesn't have to be monetary... can be a later curfew, friends over night, a 10 minute backrub, doing a chore either for them or with them, etc). Teens would greatly love parents to volunteer to do their dishes for them, or better yet, wash while the teen dries, thus spending some quality time with him/her simultaneously.

Parenting With Pizazz

I have learned in the 15 years of being a foster/adoptive parent that, contrary to parental popular belief, teens want adult interaction. There is an old adage that states "people don't care how much you know until they know how much you care." My teens have taught me, and research bears this out, that our young people need us to be actively involved in their lives thus showing them that we care by spending time with them. Having quality time with parents is of paramount importance to teens floundering in society today. They look for direction from adults who don't just "talk the talk, but walk the walk". Remembering Cats In The Cradle, the 1970's song by Harry Chapin, gives us insight as to how important it is to honor our children by giving of our time and selves.

There is a plethora of information via books and websites geared towards parenting our next generation. I can but only scratch the surface, even from my own personal experiences, when it comes to discussing parenting techniques for molding our young adults into successful societal members. However, I have seen for myself the success that can be gained by incorporating the five love languages into everyday discipline while also utilizing the Fred Sanford approach to motivating our teens to rethink the wayward direction they may be heading.

We are indeed making a positive difference in the life of our teens, so hang in there. We're all in this together.

Walk In A Manner Worthy

Ignorance Isn't Always Bliss

"You WHAT?" I exclaimed in total frustration after David told me he'd thrown his extra paper in a trash can at the city park. He had just inherited this paper route from his older foster brother a day or so earlier. Already he appeared to be shirking his responsibility to his employer and customers.

He knew he had 29 papers – the exact number of customers on the daily list attached to the bundle thrown on our doorstep. David had just returned from delivering 28 papers when I received a call from one of his missed customers. I informed him that to keep this route, I expected him to deliver ALL his papers. His excuse (which I considered lame) was that more than one of the same address existed. Already frustrated, I had a hard time hearing any excuses, especially one I knew was not true. I was seconds from making him unemployed again by bringing his carrier days to an abrupt halt. I refrained only because I wanted the 29th house to get its Saturday edition of the local newspaper before "firing" the deliverer. I kept my cool as I drove David, who by this time was frustrated also, around town hoping he would recognize the paperless home. He adamantly declared this was his last day on the job. I didn't argue with him on this point.

As we cruised town, David pointed out two houses visible from the same street corner. Both had the number 202 clearly evident above the front doors. It was at this time I realized David did not have a defiance/authority problem as I had prematurely assumed. He lacked map-reading skills. He was oblivious to the fact each house faced a differently named street. I quickly became aware I now had a teachable moment.

It took about 15 minutes to point out street signs and house numbers – to correspond them for the correct address. I drove to different intersections, stopped, and asked David to tell me on what streets we were located. I further asked him to point out several houses in the vicinity.

"If you wanted to write a letter to the people in this house, what address would you put on the envelope?" I asked. His physical affect changed for the positive when he got one, then two... then five correct addresses.

"Can I keep my route, Kim, now that I know where to deliver my papers?" His frustration had dissipated. Once more his excitement about earning money was evident. That evening as we were saying goodnight, he thanked me for showing him

Ignorance Isn't Always Bliss

how to read addresses. We discussed our emotional responses to what took place earlier. I then invited David to acknowledge, "I don't know" when he was unsure of something. I assured him it was OK to ask for help.

Less than two months later, David is still enthusiastic about his money-making opportunity. He has many plans for his not-yet-earned income. He is motivated to save and has since bought for himself a $105 bike to use for both work and play. It is obvious his self-esteem has grown.

When I reflect upon how close I was to ending this learning process that Saturday, I cringe. This experience has humbled me while yet reminding me that oftentimes it's not being "authority challenged", but being unaware, that produces attitude in our young charges. Rather than admit vulnerability, kids would rather suffer consequences for "sporting a 'tude" then to lose face with peers and those in authority. It is our job to enlighten our young people with hopes of decreasing or alleviating altogether the negative side effects of lack of knowledge. Contrary to the popular adage, ignorance is not always bliss.

Walk In A Manner Worthy

A View From The Zoo

I should have shut my camera case after last using it, but alas, I did not. As I bent over to help my 3-year-old son tie his shoe, my Pentax fell onto the hard concrete sidewalk inside the Desert Dome of Henry Doorley Zoo in Omaha, Nebraska. As I picked it up, I wondered how much abuse it could actually take before it quit working. I was to soon find out.

I finished up the last two frames taking pictures of our 13-year-old daughter putting her face through one of the little wooden comic cutouts placed near where we were resting. After the film automatically rewound, I replaced the roll, ready to continue capturing memories of our special day at the zoo. Unfortunately, as I went to shut the back of the camera, a small black, plastic piece fell into my hands. The camera had given up the ghost after the umpteenth time of unintentional mishandling by its owner.

Our rambunctious 3 year old, still full of energy after several hours of parading through the varied animal displays, was climbing on the sculptured lion near the zoo's exit when I told Diane our photo taking was done…and on the first day of our four day mini-vacation to boot. As we together gave one last ditch effort to get the camera to work, we breathed a corporate sigh of frustration at our negative turn of events. However, this was now the LEAST of our worries.

Upon putting the useless camera back into the case, we noticed Logan was no longer playing on the lion. As the crowd milled around us, our anxiety grew. WHERE WAS OUR SON???? With fear mounting within both of us, we scanned the periphery of the area leading to the parking lot. Oh God, PLEASE let us find our little boy!!

I ran to the exit gate into the parking lot expecting to find some "psycho-pervert" carrying my screaming son to a vehicle, but me being too far away to do anything about it. Just a week before, a 7 year old girl was kidnapped, raped and killed in California. No God, I don't want to make national news!

I notified the park security of our situation while describing Logan's attire and where we last saw him. Diane was still frantically searching the area where he was last seen. Nikki, too, was nervously scouting the area for her lost little brother.

Time stood still. Praying was the only thing of which I was mindful. Ten long minutes later, we got word that he had been located and was okay. Thank you, Jesus. Apparently he did not want to leave the Desert Dome and had, in the less-than-30 seconds it took us to try to fix the camera, dismounted the lion and wandered with a crowd back to see the reptilian life that was of curiosity to him. Interestingly, I had gone back there after notifying the authorities that he was missing. Going another 20 feet or so would have eased my fear, as he would have then been within eyesight.

It is remarkable what goes on in one's mind when hit with a harrowing experience such as this. My prayer was "No, God, I don't want to make national news." Diane's prayer was "God, if he is going to die, please let it be fast and not in the sick way that happened to the little girl in California". Current events color our perspective. Emotions can blind us to rational thought. Fear calmed can, much like a finger that no longer hurts after hitting it with a hammer, make us aware that much of what we have we take for granted.

I surprised myself with my afterthoughts as we ended our tour of the zoo. After thanking God profusely for keeping our son safe, my mind wandered to the arena of foster/adoptive care. Being a foster/adoptive parent, I tried to put myself in the shoes of those that have "lost" their children to the system for whatever reasons.

Regardless of what transpired prior to the taking of their children, I believe most parents have felt the "fear of the unknown" as it relates to those to whom they have given birth. Only the coldest of hearts would have no emotional struggles upon having children taken from them. Even the most inept parents fight to get visitation and keep parental rights. The most dysfunctional adults, I want to believe, wonder if their offspring are well cared for...what is happening to them throughout any given day.

As a former Iowa Department of Human Services and private agency worker (and even as a foster/adoptive parent), I have sometimes discounted and greatly minimized what it must be like emotionally for the biological parents of the kids in alternative home care. We do not know the parents of our adopted son, but were told that the final good-bye was tearful and emotional, even for the worker. Consciously aware of it or not, we have a connection with two strangers that may well be losing sleep every night, wondering if the product of their union is thriving in the home of those he now calls "Mommy and Daddy".

Our long ten minutes brought into awareness for me the fact that, in all probability, even the most hard-hearted or emotionally numbed parents are able to feel a gamut of emotions, especially as it relates to their children. Moreover, I think I've discovered within me a refined compassion toward parents with children in out-of-home placements, regardless of the reasons that got their young ones placed.

I am truly thankful that our zoo drama had a happy ending. For many parents (and children) in the system, this is not the case. May we, as foster/adoptive parents and social workers, bear in mind that "there for the grace of God, go I." We live in a sad and hurting world. A little less judgmentalism toward those for whom we frequently have little patience just might reap some wonderful rewards. Too, may he that is without sin, throw the first stone.

The Importance Of Biological Family In Foster Care/Adoption

Children in the foster care/adoption system carry invisible and very painful wounds coming in part from the separation from biological loved ones. In the thirty years I have been in the human service arena I have interacted with myriad children and adults who struggle with "who am I" as a result of being adopted, even some who were legalized into another's family as infants. There seems to be a gnawing wondering to some degree about those with whom they are related by blood. I've heard many a story, both good and bad, about finding biological family after a court's decision to terminate parental rights and a new family is subsequently found. The following is our story.

It numbers among one of the worst weekends of my life. Tears flowed freely as I anticipated telling my adopted sibling group of four that I had received word that their biological mother was dead. DNA tests confirmed that the bones found four months earlier were indeed those of their mom.

I received the call on Thursday afternoon at 4:00. My heart sank as I struggled with how to tell four children I loved so much that their dream of someday being reunited with their mother was now crushed forever. I would have to wait until Friday AM to inform them of this news since Matt, the oldest, was at work and wouldn't be home until way after the youngest were in bed. Watching the movie Pay It Forward that night only provoked more tears. My kids looked at me as if to say, "Yeah, Dad, it's a sad movie, but not *that* sad." Little did they know what was to come in less than 12 hours.

Having been a state social worker in the 80's I recalled how children in the foster care/adoption system pined for their biological parents/family. Knowing this, I had plugged my children's maternal grandmother's phone number, which the worker gave me long ago, into my cell phone for future reference. It was upon getting the call regarding [Mom's] death that I decided to risk the phone interaction at this sad time for both of us.

"You don't know me, but I am calling to tell you how sorry I am to hear of your daughter's death. I just want you to know that my wife and I have adopted four of her five children and that they are okay."

Tears came readily for both of us as she explained how she had been looking for her precious grandchildren, wondering for over half a decade if they were together... healthy...thriving wherever they might be placed. Grandmother asked permission to give my number to her youngest daughter so she could contact me also. Permission was granted. "Gramma" also informed me that there would be a memorial service for Mom on September 19, when an ordained minister uncle from Ohio would be in Iowa, as he wanted to perform the service. I let her know that we would do everything possible to be there with the kids.

During that 6 week period between the initial call and the family reunion, Matt, Jose and I met with Aunt Jackie, who was thrilled to see her nephews. She filled in many of the blanks of the boys' life for all of us. The boys were reticent on the 90-minute drive home, but content to have once again connected with a biological family member, who was gracious and very supportive of my wife and me for the keeping of her family together through adoption.

Two weeks prior to the memorial service, a cousin found through Facebook an older biological half-sister who was living with her father's mother in Texas. Gramma Mary drove from southern Texas so that the kids could be reunited once again for the remembrance of Mom. To say the day was "bittersweet" would be an understatement.

Diane and I were nervous as we undertook this emotional event. However, upon receiving the hugs and many "thank yous" from those that were genuinely grateful that the children landed in a Christian home where parents were so willing to allow them contact with blood relatives, our fears were relieved.

Gramma Mary and their sister, Crystal, drove to our home for supper that night. There was not a dry eye in the place as the kids said goodbyes, not knowing when they would see each other again. We vowed to keep in touch.

Fast forward 6 months. Matt, being 16, struggled with the "who am I" question. He was restless here and needed to find himself. Thus, Gramma Mary, Diane and I agreed that Matt would go to Texas for an indefinite period of time when school released for the summer. I told Matt I loved him enough to "let him go". The months prior to him leaving were difficult, at best, between the two of us. Separation anxiety reared its ugly head. It's easier to leave when everyone is angry with each other...a phenomenon that I have seen repeatedly in my human service career.

The Importance Of Biological Family In Foster Care/Adoption

Matt left in June for a new chapter in his life...and ours. It was difficult, fearing Matt would grow to love his biological family more than he loved us, and thus perhaps choose to stay in Texas. I was many times on my knees in prayer for him during his absence.

My family was able to take an extended vacation in October to stay with Matt and his family down South. It had been 4 months since we had seen him and didn't have much contact with him prior to that time (I gave him his space as I told him I would). We discovered a new maturity in Matt since he left Iowa. As much as he loved his bio family there, he wanted to come back with us, but knew that wasn't possible and still keep the credits he needed to graduate on time here in Iowa.

Matt returned to our home in March last year. The nine months he was gone helped refocus his priorities. He realized that "family" was more than just a blood connection – the emotional connection was of significance also. His stint in Texas was a great experience for him and drew us closer, rather than apart, as I had initially imagined. Matt has developed into a very fine young adult in whom Diane and I are quite proud.

We continue to keep in touch with family here in Iowa and in Texas. Crystal, now 20, is planning a trip to Iowa this spring. We look forward to her visit...again enhancing the biological connection between siblings, which we have seen to have healing properties. Iowa grandmother and aunt are involved with us, as is family in Texas, supporting us when things get rough as they sometimes do.

As a follower of Jesus, I trust God's word, and have seen it play out..."all things work together for good for those that love the Lord and are called according to His purpose." (Romans 8:28) The tragedy of Mom's death was not an end, but a beginning...the beginning of some healing that might not have otherwise taken place in the hearts of my children.

I think the signature line on Matt's thank you letter to Iowa Gramma for the $50 Wal-Mart card he received for Christmas speaks volumes, not just from our 18 year old adoptee, but for many who have been separated from families:

"Love you forever and always!! – Matti"

Walk In A Manner Worthy

Connecting With Birth Parents

Years ago I realized that of all the parents I've had the privilege to work with, not one do I believe ever woke up one morning in their youth thinking "I am going to have babies someday just so I could royally mess up their young lives. Yessirreebob, that's what I aspire to...messing up children's lives." It is preposterous to believe that anyone would conceive of such a notion, yet somewhere between conception and the wounds wrought after birth, something went terribly askew.

I've been in the human service profession for almost three decades in various capacities...DHS social worker, in-home worker, therapist in a residential treatment facility, case manager and, on top of all this, now have five awesome adopted children after having fostered 35+ teenage boys in the last 14 years. I have learned much from the parents and children with whom I have interacted.

Back in the 80's I had a foster mom tell me "all of us are only 15 minutes away from a child abuse allegation." It wasn't until I became a foster parent in May of '94 that I understood this, and thought she overestimated by about 14 minutes. I would bet there is at least one reader that can attest to days where stress was so overwhelming that thoughts of, at minimum, verbal assault on children were not entertained, if not acted upon. Yet how many of us have prematurely judged a biological parent of one of the young charges in our care without ever having walked a mile in his/her shoes.

Perhaps if we had experienced the life of any of those parents the question "why are you like you are?" Would turn to "why aren't you worse?" I am frequently reminded that even as much as I've been blessed, I have had to ask forgiveness from my kids or clients because I responded to their choices in a less-than-mature way. And if I can respond incorrectly given the pretty cushy life I've had in comparison to those with whom I've worked, how much harder it must be to be patient for those that have endured horrendous experiences at the hand of adults in their young lives.

Now before anyone starts thinking I am excusing acts of physical/sexual abuse or denial of critical care, I just want to state for the record that I am not. I am merely suggesting that perhaps we should try to see life through the eyes of the biological parents and thus maybe find that their hearts aren't as black as we initially believed. I've discovered that as I've humbled myself before these hurting individuals I have learned much from them in spite of their failure to raise children in such a manner as to avoid "the system."

Connecting With Birth Parents

So how do we then connect with these very important people, those that have given life to the kids we love? It begins, for me, with praying that I can see them with God's eyes and with His love. It is hard not to find something to like and admire as we pray blessings upon people with whom we now have a common bond...our children. Finding common ground is my first goal when meeting and getting to know parents. It is fairly easy to hone into commonality if one visits the parental home. I anticipated finding conversation starters as I looked around the dwelling...from taste in furniture, pictures hanging on the wall, books on the coffee tables or anything else I could glean from a scan of their living environment.

As a foster parent, I requested that team meetings be held in our home where parents could visualize where their children are living (yes, I know that this isn't always possible for various reasons, but probably more so than is actually happening). I've also tried to get the parent(s) to tell me as much about the young person as I could. Birthdays, anniversaries, wedding dates, etc. were also venues for connecting. Would it not warm your heart if a bio parent would call you on your birthday to wish you a very special day??? Chances are good it would...and thus a call or card to a bio parent can also help bridge emotional gaps in the relationship if things aren't going so well.

A very special friend of mine in Tennessee whom I call "Mom" told me a story of how she finally connected with the very distant and cold biological mother of one of her youngsters. Betty taught this particular young man how to cook. Mom would come get the boy for visitations, but would not talk to nor look at Betty during the pickup/drop off times. Yet Betty continued to attempt a connection, seemingly to no avail. However, when the boy went home with his mother, he would show her what Betty had taught him in the kitchen. Over time, this mom was so impressed with what Betty taught her son that her heart warmed to the degree Betty received a verbal THANK YOU from this formerly cold and aloof woman.

Shortly after Diane and I started fostering a sibling group of four, their mother did visits in our home. On one particular visit, I was speaking with Mom in our kitchen and told her that I thought she had awesome kids and had done a great job teaching her children manners and courtesy toward others. Mom started crying, telling me that no one had ever told her that before and then asked for a hug. She wept many tears onto my shoulder as I "parented" her, comforting her as a father would comfort a hurting daughter. I had no idea at that time this act of kindness towards her would majorly impact my life.

Walk In A Manner Worthy

The termination hearing was held a few weeks later. The judge ruled for Mom's termination of parental rights. We later adopted her four children. Last August it was discovered that bones found in a wooded area in April 2007 were those of my kids' biological mother who had been missing for over 3 years. I telephoned Mom's mother whom I had never met nor spoken with before, telling her of the adoption of her four grandchildren and my sadness at the news of the loss of her daughter. It was indeed a bittersweet day for Grandmother...hearing of daughter's death, but having good news of grandchildren after trying to locate them for nearly 5 years. Because of my interaction with Mom 3 years earlier, Grandmother was able to be excited for where her kin was placed because Mom reported that they were in a good Christian home with parents that loved them. This was one of the last messages Grandmother received from her biological, now deceased loved one.

It is hard for me to type this without getting teary again. Had Diane and I not had a heart for the biological parent with whom we've shared children, Mom may have gone to her grave unsure and insecure about her children's welfare and future. But because we strived to love her as God would have us do, Mom...and extended family...knew their kids were loved and in a protective home.

Yes, Mom made some unwise and poor choices. However, in the midst of those, I believe she loved her children the best she knew how given the hurt she carried around from bad things that happened in her life. There are many parents I have grown to respect and admire through the trials and tribulations that brought me into their lives. I now know that social workers, foster/adoptive parents, teachers and others in our children's lives can help heal the hearts of those who, by no fault of their own, were disrupted from their family of origin. We can reach out in love to those who have lost their children for various reasons. I have done this and have thus found that I was sometimes in the presence of angels unaware. The Bible, my anchor in life, tells me that if I do anything for the "least of these", I do it for Him. Take courage then as we love the "unlovable" for the Bible also tells us that "our labor in the Lord is not in vain" (I Cor 15:58). May He be glorified in all that we do.

Connecting With Birth Parents

Since this story was originally written, Mom's mother, along with four other family members, visited the Combes home to see the four siblings. The visit went well and was healing for all involved. I received the following email upon Grandmother's return home:

> Thank you so very much, more than words can say, for the best day I have had in years, literally...I do believe I will get less emotional as time goes on, it's just that I know how deeply she loved them, and she is not here to be with them..I will do better, it's just that they are all I have left of her... please tell Diane how very much we appreciate that she put up with the extra work, on top of all that she already has...we commented all the way home how good we felt, what a wonderful time we all had, and how perfect the day was, and it really was..well dear man, I will close for now, tell the kids to call any time, I would love that. I love you all,
>
> Grandma

Walk In A Manner Worthy

Father's Day Letter

Yet another FOSTERING FAMILIES TODAY submission. This letter was never sent, but very heartfelt.

June 18, 2000 (Father's Day)

Dear Jackie and Joe (real names as Logan is hoping a relative will read this and tell his parents to contact us),

It is with much thankfulness to God that I write this letter to you on this special day. My wife and I wanted you to know that because of you, we have a most wonderful blessing that fills our hearts with love and delight.

My wife was unable to bear children at the time we got married. Complications arose and a hysterectomy became necessary. Her inability to conceive brought on a depression that put a damper on her joy of life. When we were told that a baby was available for adoption, she immediately jumped at this opportunity. I, on the other hand, did initially not want babies in my life. It was fine with me that no babies could be produced as a result of our union. However, to give my wife the desire of her heart, I agreed to meet with the worker and foster parents, and of course, Logan. Here's what happened.

When I saw the worker come into the room with a small bundle of blanket in her arms, I met them at the door. I took Logan from her arms, looked at him, and tears streamed down my cheeks. God gave me an instant bond with the baby you two created. What an absolutely beautiful little boy. I think I let Diane hold him about 10 minutes the first 24 hours he was in our home. I held him, prayed for him, and cried joyful tears for the wonderful gift Jesus gave us. Even now as I type, tears are welling as I watch our son play in my office as his new "Da-da" types this letter to his biological parents.

Joe and Jackie, we want you to know that we will always let Logan know the gift you gave him…a new life. At the time of his birth, you were unable to best meet his needs. He will know how hard it was for you to let him go to another family. He will see the pictures the worker took of your last good-bye in March 2000. He will know he was loved by both of you. Rest assured, he is in a Christian home and greatly loved.

Father's Day Letter

If you will let the private agency workers know your whereabouts, we will continue to send you updates and pictures at least once a year so you can see the progress your son is making. If you would like to send letters, we will put them away for him until such a time he is able to understand and appreciate your decision to relinquish parental rights at this juncture of your lives. If, as he approaches his late teen years and early adulthood, he would like to meet you (and you are open to this also), we would seriously consider allowing him to do this. We have no problem with him knowing you and having involvement with you at that time, as long as it is healthy for him to do so.

Thank you again for your heart-wrenching decision. We are praying for you and will continue to do so. We don't know you, but you are and always will be, a very significant part of our lives. We share the privilege of loving the same little boy. May God comfort your hearts and give you His peace as you think about this precious gift of our mutual son.

With much gratitude to you and God,

Logan's adoptive parents

Walk In A Manner Worthy

Adverse Childhood Experiences

"Trauma changes the biology of the brain, but just ONE loving, secure, and nurturing relationship also changes the biology of the brain." – Dr. Bruce Perry

Dr. Perry is my "rock star" in the human service field. He and his researchers are on the cutting edge of investigating children with PTSD, and how it affects those who have come from very difficult and traumatic backgrounds. In fact, I utilize his materials in my own presentations which are geared toward foster/adoptive parents, social workers, teachers, day care providers and others – all of whom have children with difficult and challenging behaviors in their charge.

Having been in the counseling arena in some capacity or another for over three and a half decades, I can confirm the veracity of the above quote. Research has shown tangible evidence of the heinous results of trauma…relationships that have been marred by such things as neglect, physical and sexual abuse, domestic violence and substance abuse in children's lives.

MRI scans clearly show brain dysfunction in those with multiple ACEs (Adverse Childhood Experiences), pictures that resemble the "dark side of the moon" with black crater-like imaging throughout. However, when the same child is placed in a thriving environment in as little time as 6 months to a year, with all needs being met, an MRI photo will start showing bright colors – reds, purples, etc., displaying areas where healing is taking place and synapses are connecting in healthy ways.

It was formerly thought that once a brain was damaged, repair was not an option. Studies have since conclusively shown that previous thinking was in error. For example, my wife and I took our adoptive toddler son (born to parents both having intellectual disabilities) to a geneticist 17 years ago. It was thought by the placing social workers that Logan had some "syndrome," the name of which I can no longer remember. Tests came back negative, thankfully, but I will always remember what the examining doctor told Diane and me. "You cannot change the hard drive a baby is born with, but you can enhance that hard drive by the software you put into it." Wow, the validity of Dr. Perry's research, reworded in computer terminology.

As our son grew we did our best to stimulate and challenge his brain while providing for him a safe and nurturing home environment. Now, at 17½ years of age, he has already exceeded the prognosis we were given from professionals when we received him in our family at 10½ months old. His brain, before he was removed

Adverse Childhood Experiences

from his biological parents at 3 months, was in "failure to thrive" mode. Neglect of his basic needs so early on did indeed negatively affect him. Left for hours in a car seat by his caregivers, with very little or no stimulation, brought him close to death before DHS could place him in foster care. The software we installed upon his entrance into our family, did not completely reverse what genes and history did to his command center, but he is much further along than what genes and traumatic history would have initially dictated.

My son's story is just one of a myriad stories I've heard from others or have experienced firsthand over the course of my career. While PTSD undeniably has severe consequences on children enduring tumultuous and chaotic situations, the outcomes do not have to be all gloom and doom. One does not have to be psychologically savvy to do profound work in helping overcome ACEs. Anyone can be audaciously present in a youngster's life, thus creating an environment of hope and a legacy of love for those who desperately need both.

Walk In A Manner Worthy

If You Only Knew What I Know

I read this on Facebook four years ago. Because of our son, Logan, this resonated with me.

Dear Woman in Target-

I've heard it before, you know. That I "spoil that baby". You were convinced that she'd never learn to be "independent". I smiled at you, kissed her head, and continued my shopping.

If you only knew what I know.

If you only knew how she spent the first ten months of her life utterly alone inside a sterile metal crib, with nothing to comfort her other than sucking her fingers.

If you only knew what her face looked like the moment her orphanage caregiver handed her to me to cradle for the very first time--fleeting moments of serenity commingled with sheer terror. No one had ever held her that way before, and she had no idea what she was supposed to do.

If you only knew that she would lay in her crib after waking and never cry--because up until now, no one would respond.

If you only knew that anxiety was a standard part of her day, along with banging her head on her crib rails and rocking herself for sensory input and comfort.

If you only knew that this baby in the carrier is heartbreakingly "independent" --and how we will spend minutes, hours, days, weeks, months, and years trying to override the part of her brain that screams "trauma" and "not safe."

If you only knew what I know.

If you only knew that this baby now whimpers when she's put down instead of when she is picked up.

If you only knew that this baby "sings" at the top of her lungs in the mornings and after her nap, because she knows that her chatter will bring someone to lift her out of her crib and change her diaper.

If you only knew that this baby rocks to sleep in her Mama's or her Papa's arms instead of rocking herself.

If You Only Knew What I Know

If you only knew that this baby made everyone cry the day she reached out for comfort, totally unprompted.

If you only knew what I know.

"Spoiling that baby" is the most important job I will ever have, and it is a privilege. I will carry her for a little while longer--or as long as she'll let me--because she is learning that she is safe. That she belongs. That she is loved.

If you only knew..

FACEBOOK, Kelly Dirkes (April 25, 2016)

Walk In A Manner Worthy

We Can All Make A Difference

The phone call came the Thursday before a long holiday weekend in 1996.

"Could I speak with Kim, please?"

"This is he."

"Kim, you may not remember me, but you worked at [local residential treatment center] when I was in your cottage. This is Will."

"WILL!!!!????!! Yes, I remember you. Where are you?"

"I am going to be in Iowa over the weekend. We are returning late Monday afternoon and I was wondering...if you were going to be around...could we get together? I want you to meet my wife and kids. Would this be OK?"

My mind raced backwards to April 1983. Will had been a difficult 14 year old resident in Pine Cottage and had been discharged due to physical aggression toward staff and peers. For whatever reasons, prior to his leaving Will and I had established a rapport that seemed stronger than that between myself and the other residents [RT center] was serving at that time. I always wondered what happened to Will. Did he work through his issues, was he "successfully" living life within socially acceptable perimeters?

I excitedly looked forward to Monday evening. How did he now look? What topics would our conversation include? Would the rapport still be there over so much time? I soon found out. He was taller, heavier and had less hair than when I last saw him, but there was no doubt this was the now-grown resident whom God had 13 years earlier allowed me to see through His eyes. As I extended my hand in greeting I was met with an unexpected hug that conveyed much warmth and affection that seemed to have been saved up over many years.

Our time together "catching up" flew by quickly. I met his family. We shared our lives. I shared my faith. Four hours and four pizzas later, good-byes were said with a non-verbal "let's-not-wait-another-13-years-to-do-this-again" tone. Whether we will ever again connect is yet to be seen. Regardless, an impact had been made...on both of us.

We Can All Make A Difference

In the exuberance of youthful thinking back in my early 20's and as a young Christian who wanted to reach the world for Jesus, I desired as a residence counselor in a home for emotionally challenged youth to touch the lives of hurting children, hoping to be a positive change agent in their lives. In my attempt to reflect Christ's love to these young people, I know I failed to always respond in Christ-like ways to the myriad manifested misbehaviors demanding my attention. I realized that I "shot from the hip" when these kids tested me in their own unique ways. I was unsure how to adequately respond when they acted out their internal turmoil. After talking with Will, I am convinced that it is not an adult's weaknesses/failures children remember most. They are willing and quick to forgive if they sense a genuine care and concern from those in authority who treat them with respect and dignity. I also learned that my actions and words had impacted him more than what I imagined. Evidence of this came as Will reported to me things I said and did of which I had no recollection. Surprisingly, these things left an impression that went beyond anything I might have purposefully planned to instill in his young heart and mind.

"You guys listen to him. He knows what he's talking about" were his parting words to the four young men with whom I was sharing my home as a foster parent. They, of course, rolled their eyes to indicate their playful "Yeah, right" attitude as they looked at me, smiling.

I had just received the ultimate compliment. A former agency client acknowledging that I had some semblance of wisdom, encouraging the next generation to heed my words and actions. Oh, that we who desire to help others, in and out of the human service field, could see and hear this much more often. But I won't be greedy. I will thank my Heavenly Father, take these compliments when I can get them and soak them up. Every last drop.

Walk In A Manner Worthy

A Birthday Blessing

 I totally concur with those that espouse the evils of Facebook (and other social media venues) as I've seen first-hand the drama and hurtful narrative that inundates my thread feed on a weekly, if not daily basis. That said, however, it is always my desire to utilize my page to lovingly challenge worldviews and to encourage the sad and hurting by bringing humor in the form of jokes and puns to those who have chosen to be my "friends."

 The following is an example of why I continue to enjoy Facebook even given the darkness one can surely glean from even a cursory reading of the messages posted on our walls. This is but one example of how God can use Facebook to make such a huge impact in a person's life - like He did on a just-turned 12 year old girl and her family.

 As I scrolled through my thread on July 24, 2019 a friend had posted something that caused great compassion (and frustration) for her. Angela, a colleague in the field, saw a posting from a foster/adoptive parent on social media. Being a foster/adoptive parent herself, she is sensitive to such situations, as she describes below:

> "Today a friend held a birthday party for her child. Some weeks ago Mom sent out 10 or 12 invitations. Five declined for various reasons. The remaining invitees did not respond. Mom reached out again a day or 2 ago to those who had not responded. Still nothing. Today was the birthday party. Guess what. Not one child showed up. I can't stop thinking about the heartbreak of that child. Waiting in anticipation of their guests arriving watching out the window and watching the time tick by. This is why we don't do friend parties for our kids. Shame on the parents. Each one was directly informed and invited by the mom and did not have the courtesy to reply much less show up. I am angry and heartbroken for my friend and her child."

 I am all too familiar with the emotions that come in situations like this. We, too, have had similar experiences and the subsequent heartbreak of watching a little heart crushed when the anticipated activities did not come to fruition. Also, as a human service worker, I had this scenario play out numerous times with clients whose own parents did not follow through with promises of special activities or gifts to celebrate their child being another year older.

 Being moved myself, I decided to copy and paste my friend's post to my own wall,

A Birthday Blessing

reminding friends to please be courteous by RSVPing to parties when invited rather than just choose not to show up causing such hurt to a child looking forward to celebrating a special event with friends. In so doing, I received a private message from a young lady I met a decade earlier while volunteering to work a Teens Encounter Christ weekend in which my son, Jose, was involved. Katey informed me that the 12 year old girl so hurt by no one attending her party was her adopted sister. Shortly thereafter I got a message from Katey's mother whom I had also met through a training several years prior.

I did not expect to have known the family nor did I expect the number of responses and comments I got for this particular post. The story seemed to trigger readers who experienced various degrees of disappointment and hurt somewhere in their own past. One friend, Ashley, decided to brainstorm in the comments about how to turn this otherwise dismal situation into a party for this young lady after all. It was her suggestion to invite all my Facebook friends interested in doing so to send cards and letters to the birthday girl, hoping to change her despair to joy as mail would trickle into her home over the next few days.

What an awesome idea! I asked Mom via Messenger if this would be okay and she thus gave me the address to which people could send best wishes. Hope was resurrected in a hurting mother's heart. She believed her daughter would be overwhelmed with the outpouring of love coming from total strangers.

Next, as if this wasn't already enough, God, in His love for this depressed birthday girl, prompted a 27 year old avid motorcycle rider to pursue me for yet another blessing for this family. Caleb was one of my son, Matt's, best friends in middle school and beyond. Caleb frequented our house off and on growing up. Life had thrown Caleb a few one-two punches in his early years, all of which softened his heart towards others whom he perceived as downtrodden. Between becoming bitter or better, Caleb chose "better." His idea for helping actually got me teary. I PMed Katey's mom and bounced the idea off her. She was overjoyed and wrote that if I trusted Caleb, she, too, would trust him.

Caleb drew together a handful of his 2-wheeling friends to ride over an hour to surprise the birthday girl with a motorcycle parade where she would be the Grand Marshall for the day. The ride couldn't take place until a couple weeks past her birth date so Mom kept all the cards and letters that came pouring in so as to have a doubly huge surprise when Caleb and his friends arrived.

Walk In A Manner Worthy

Being out of state on the set date, I was unable to be in attendance but I did see pictures and postings on other friends' walls, friends that didn't know the family, but wanted to be involved in surprising this pre-teen after the pain of an epic fail birthday party two weeks prior. No surprise to those who know me personally, I shed tears of joy upon seeing pictures and hearing of this phenomenal day of surprises. I could not have been more proud of Caleb for his loving action. He gathered friends to ride 60 miles one way to take a discouraged birthday girl out for ice cream while allowing her to ride proudly on a cycle with someone who absolutely made the previous disaster tolerable.

Scripture reads in Romans 8:28 "all things work together for good for those who love the Lord and are called according to His purpose." This family, who adopted a girl who needed love, did so to fulfill their Christian ministry to love "orphans" and widows which the Bible instructs believers to do. These parents, hard as it was to endure the vicarious pain of rejection of their charge, trusted God to work "immeasurable above and beyond all they could ask or even imagine."

Caleb, unbeknownst to him at the time, was the conduit through which God worked. I later informed him that Jesus used him to heap love on this girl that needed so badly to know that people cared...that God cared...for her. Ashley's idea prompted the string of events leading to the ride and Caleb generously topped it all off. I am so thankful to them, and to all who sent cards and gifts to a young lady who will never forget her 12th birthday and the emotional rollercoaster ride surrounding it.

Because I wanted to share this story in the pages you're reading, I asked Caleb to author a brief synopsis of this event from his perspective, which he gladly did:

> "I did the motorcycle ride to make [her] feel loved and special as she should have felt on her actual birthday. I was a couple weeks late, but I thought it was better late than never. Hearing her story sadden my heart. I couldn't imagine going through something like that at such a young age.
>
> It was a very exciting moment for me that day. Seeing her face light up and seeing how shocked she was to see all of us and our bikes. I felt at that moment that I made a difference. It was one of the coolest feelings I have ever had. I hope when she gets older, she still remembers that 12th birthday and how she felt that day." – Caleb Daggett

A Birthday Blessing

As one can glean from this reading, it doesn't take an act of Congress to make a difference in someone's life. I thank God for allowing me to be the catalyst for all that transpired. But obviously, I could never have done this on my own, even if I had been the one to think of all the "connect the dots" that came from Ashley and Caleb. So...thank you, Ashley and thanks Caleb. Loveya, Man!!!

Walk In A Manner Worthy

Journey With Jason

"WILL YOU ABANDON ME?" These words haunted me well into the holiday season following the initial meeting of my future foster son, a young man with no perceived security or stability in his 16-year-old life. In an ideal world, this question would never have passed his lips.

It was in July '95 that I was first made aware of Jason. Because of my experience as a human service worker and a foster parent, his juvenile court officer believed that my personality might best match with the problems this teen may manifest in my home, should I choose to foster this challenging client. He was currently placed in a residential facility, needing to work its program before he could graduate, be discharged and placed in my foster home. His juvenile court officer would keep me posted on his progress.

Jason wanted to meet me after hearing there was a foster parent potentially willing to have him in his home. A staffing was held on November 16. The juvenile court officer drove Jason's mother (who he had not seen in over a year) and me to the facility. While making conversation during the 3½ hour one-way drive, I realized that I had met Jason's extended family several years ago while employed with the Iowa Department of Human Services. His mother and I concluded it was a small world.

Upon seeing his mother, Jason hugged her and wanted her close to him as the assembly of social workers and treatment staff gathered to discuss his progress. He watched me intently, seemingly trying to get a grasp on who I was. Was I someone to be trusted? When the reporting was done regarding Jason's behaviors he was given an opportunity to "interview" me. His longing look, coupled with his first words, tugged at my heartstrings. His inquiry underscored his first and foremost priority. Rather than delve for information regarding rules, home life, brothers and other related issues, his most predominate concern popped out with no apparent effort - "Will you abandon me?" His affect disguised the vulnerability underlying the words. What if I said YES (or couldn't convince him I wouldn't)? He wanted to trust, but history was not on his side. Why should he believe I would be different than others to whom he had given his susceptible heart?

I can't remember my response to this pointed and poignant request for a "forever" relationship. The intensity of it took me aback. I had been in the human service arena for over 15 years. I thought I had seen and heard it all. However, in this con-

Journey With Jason

text, I could not rid myself of the echoing memory of those four powerful words. It was as if I held his life in the balance.

Jason spent some time with me and the foster siblings in my home over Thanksgiving and New Year's holidays during his pre-placement visits. He was anxious to graduate so he could then become a member of my household and family. This was not to happen until February 12th, however. It was then that his still-echoing words were going to be put to the test.

He initially hated the court-ordered day treatment program in which he was placed. This program provided him some structure so he could more easily transition into having the freedom most teens his age have. Because he had been in a locked facility for so long, he would need some bridge to insure a smoother changeover into the real world again. The frustration of having to spend 12 hours a day in another therapeutic environment, coupled with the influence of a negative foster brother, sparked the explosive combination of ingredients that was a recipe for trouble.

Within five weeks of placement in my home, he bolted from his court-ordered structure. He was found within two weeks and subsequently spent a month in a short-term group facility. Tearfully he asked me over the phone if he was able to return to my home. "Most assuredly so," I told him.

Six months and many power struggles later, he was once more placed in a short-term facility for "regroup time" due to some poor decision making on his part. A visit and several phone calls again gave him the confidence that I was still there and still FAMILY. He was placed back with me for round three.

Fall turned into winter. Jason began to trust that I was committed to his well-being...and to HIM. Progress was being made. Jason's increasing maturity was reflected in his making better life choices and decisions. His desire to be reunited with his Mom grew stronger as they spent time together getting reacquainted. They had been separated for various reasons for much of his short life.

Winter gave way to spring--a season of rebirth. It would seem appropriate, then, that this season of positive growth and change would see Jason back with his mom full-time. It was an emotional moment when his worker remarked at a monthly team meeting that she saw no reason for him to stay in foster care. He and his mom were speechless as tears streamed down their cheeks. They had not anticipated this reunification until summer at the earliest. Jason was to see his hopes realized.

Walk In A Manner Worthy

Prior to leaving my home, Jason gave me his good-bye letter. The following is an excerpt from this touching farewell:

> "I do not know how to thank you so much. I came in here thinking that this was going to be another foster home that will abandon me and not help me much with anything. You have worked with my mom and I so much and helping us to get back together soon because you always told me that you would bring up to [the worker] to have me move in with her at the beginning of the summer and it happened sooner than we both thought. I think you did a very good thing for becoming a foster parent for many kids. God must have said to you at an early age to help out all these kids because they need a home to go to and a loving foster parent like yourself."

As with many things in life, desire alone does not always make dreams come true. It eventually became apparent that familial love was not enough to make this long awaited living situation work. Jason once more entered into my home. He hadn't lost the trust of our relationship after eight months of living elsewhere. We were thus able to continue to build on the pre-existing foundation we had both struggled hard to cement over the last 2 years.

The holidays once more came and went. Jason would be 18 in six months and was biting at the bit to be independent. Being on his own was priority for him. However, he wanted it to happen NOW. Thus, in tribute to Martin Luther King, Jr's birthday, he ran "free at last"...for one night. He was found and placed in detention over the holiday weekend. Yes, in answer to his question, he could come back. But, he was told by his workers and me that should he decide to abscond again (and be caught) he would spend the remainder of his minor years in lock-up to keep him safe until he reached the age of majority.

This did not deter Jason's obsession with freedom. His final break occurred on March 4th, almost four months before his 18th birthday. It wasn't until mid-May that he found either the courage or desire to call me. However, he was initially deceptive regarding his whereabouts for fear of losing the freedom he had enjoyed the last two months (and wanted to keep until the end of June, when Juvenile Court would no longer have jurisdiction).

It was during this conversation that his assumption was validated--he was still my "son" and running away again had not broken that bond. I did give him a parental chewing, but past that he felt secure in his relationship with me. He reassured

Journey With Jason

me that he didn't run because of me, but because he wanted independence and a chance to be with extended family while he was still "a kid".

It is now mid-July. Jason is almost a month into adulthood. He has come back from his uncle's ranch in South Dakota and spent a night and a day with me. He calls me 'Kim' but refers to me as his Dad when speaking with others. What an honor that is!

It's not been an easy road for either of us. Nothing of value really is. The father-son relationship was borne with tears and great frustration on both sides. But this young man now knows the answer to his long-ago asked question.

This is not unlike the Father-son relationship between God and His people. How many of us have asked the eternal question "God, will you abandon me?" I, too, have been the rebellious prodigal son. I have wanted my "freedom", not wanting to follow biblical rules. I have run away from the Lord more times than I care to admit. My Father continues to love me, protect me, and delight in my "sonship" role with Him.

PS. This note, not a part of the original published article, came to me from Jason several months past his 18th birthday:

"Thank you for never abandoning me, Dad. It has always been deep down in my heart that you are my lifesaver and I could not have done it without you. No matter the situation you were always there and no one has ever done that for me. I owe my life to you because if it was not for you I would be dead or in prison or deep into drugs that I would not know what to do. I'm glad God brought you to me and I praise Him every day for that. I LOVE YOU, DAD and that will never change... you have my promise.

LOVE ALWAYS!

YOUR SON,

Jason"

Walk In A Manner Worthy

The following is a story I specifically requested for the purpose of this book from one of our former foster sons (edited to some degree by me for publication, but still mostly in his own words). JoJo, as we affectionately called him, was a truly remarkable young man. You will read of his abuse and redemption in the next few pages. Joe continues to call periodically to give me updates on his life, his prison ministry and to pray with me. He is an amazing "ashes to beauty" reflection of the power of love.

It was New Year's Day a few years ago when we first heard from Joe in over a decade. We did not hesitate to take the collect call from him. How exciting it was to hear his voice and to catch up even for a very short time. He recalled memories from living in our home. He told of accepting the Lord and further stated that since doing so he "felt freer in prison than he ever did on the outs." He thanked us profusely for pouring into his life and into the lives of others. He wanted us to know of the profound impact we made in his life. It was a great way to start the first day of a new year.

Please, DO NOT EVER minimize the seeds planted in even the most hardened of hearts. It may take years to see the sprouting and complete fruit of what was planted, but nothing is impossible to the Creator of our universe who made man in His image for relationship. I pray this story will give you what you need to keep plowing through the hurt, fear, shame and trauma of any kind. You are indeed making a difference in the life of someone who needs you. Read on.

JoJo's Story

My name is Joseph Kope, AKA JoJo to those who are close to me. I'm 36 years old and currently serving a life sentence in the NC State Prison system. Not exactly a normal guy or in a normal place. This is not a success story in terms of the world but definitely a victory for God.

I come from an abusive home – both physical and drug abuse. The drugs were an escape for me, which only made things worse. As a troubled youth, I lived with lies and violence. I learned at 12 that my father killed himself and that my whole life was a lie. I lost my identity and thus rebelled to the extreme with drug use. Subsequently, I was sent to meet my mother who had 3 young children at the time.

So now I'm in a strange place several states away with people I didn't know and frankly, at that time, did not want to know based on the lies I was previously told.

JoJo's Story

This new placement soon disrupted when my biological mother tried to be a parent. I had no structure in my grandparent's home where I was living prior to the Iowa move, so being expected to follow new rules did not go over well with me. I soon found myself in and out of youth facilities across the state. I eventually landed in a shelter in Ames. My caseworker told me one day that she found a family with whom I could be placed in foster care. At my age with my problems I had no worries that a family would want me. Sure enough that man came to visit, but he took another guy home that day; he told me he'd be back the next for me. True to his word he did come back to take me to his home.

I know this is where most foster care stories go south but this was something new to me. I was welcomed by all the family and ended up sitting up late telling my story to this man. He never stopped listening and never interrupted me, just took it all in. Later he told of how things were run in his home. The big change for me was that we were expected to go to church as a family. I had little or no experience with church or God or even good people up until now. Of course I went to church to check it out. I didn't like it much. But this family would answer all my questions and pray for me, or with me, depending upon my opinion of God at the time.

I was respected in this home, treated like a son. The kids that were not in foster care liked me, accepted me and even looked up to me I think. I soon became trusted. They took me to meet their parents and included me in general family gatherings. Too, they got me my driver's permit.

So while all this good is going on I'm having serious inner struggles on some pretty big issues. Family, God, my desire to be free. Again, this man would stay up late to talk with me about my issues and not get mad at my fears and confusion. He would occasionally briefly rub the top of my head in a compassionate, fatherly way and pray with me, even when I didn't know what to pray for. His wife was always open to help me, too. I felt this life was too good for me. This man and his wife whom I am proud to call my parents are Kim and Diane Combes.

Unwisely, I chose to run away from what I believe was the best opportunity I ever had in my life. I ultimately ended in big trouble some years later. However, both Kim and Diane had spoken for me in my defense telling my attorney the positive things they had seen in me. I believe God used them to not only save my life but to bring me to the faith.

I did not go to the Lord right then but all those late night talks about God and

Walk In A Manner Worthy

trips to church came back to mind when I was facing the death penalty alone with no family, friends or hope..the same way I was when I first met Kim and Diane.

So in conclusion what I want to convey is that my foster care experience in a Christian home may not have seemed ideal to my young rebelling mind, but those properly administered lessons were the seed planted by Christian foster parents that grew in me. Those words and lessons came to my aid in my darkest moment and during my overwhelming struggle. They molded me into the man I am today, a strong Christian in a place where we are the absolute minority. One has to work hard daily to live a Christian life where prisoners and staff persecute those who profess Christ.

With a life sentence on my shoulders and being incarcerated for 18 years, including jail time, I can now wake up every day with a smile on my face and live my day for God. Most men in my situation feel life is a total loss and spiral into violence, depression or into any of several dysfunctional states of mental health.

I have been blessed with a guardian angel here in prison as well. Ms. Myrtle Wickham, a solid Christian lady, has been my mentor and mother figure inside these walls for 15 years. She is in her 80's and loves the Lord. Myrtle has, like Kim and Diane, been a huge factor in my life - never giving up on the man God would have me to be. Too, 6 years ago God answered my only prayer for all these years (a personal prayer) to have a family of my own. God brought me my beautiful wife-to-be and two children. Sheena's my fiancé. Her two children, Samara and Jackson are 13 and 4. I am currently working on my case with pro bono attorneys who believe I should not have gotten this sentence given the circumstances of my crime. I pray to be home soon. God is God and all things are possible through Him. I'm a living testament to God's redeeming power.

With that story you just read, sent to me by Joe, was the following letter written to me:

Kim,

JoJo's Story

I truly believe that I am the man I am today - kind, God-fearing and faithful - because of the very fact that you and Diane opened your home and heart to me. A throw-away by society's standards and worse in the eyes of the system. You made me believe there is hope for people like me. Your family made me feel alive and welcome and have since been the basis of my search in life. Only one other thing has ever felt close to the love, trust, respect and fulfillment I had in your home and it took me years to look back and see that they are one and the same - God, THE God that was reflected in your home and in your lives. The God who comforted me and made me feel like I never had before. It was the God whom I later found in the darkness of my cell all alone with no hope. So thank you for believing in me. I'm proud to have lived under your roof and especially under your rules (God's rules). I love you, Man, and miss our conversations.

Thank you both for being a light in a dark place and being a critical stop in my journey of life. Without that short stay I am positive I would not be a believer or probably even alive today. Thanks for the bread crumbs you gave me (just like in Hansel and Gretel) they led me home to the Master of my life, Jesus Christ.

Peace and blessings and all my prayers,

JoJo

To Joe (when he reads this book):

We love you. When you get out, you know we want to continue a relationship with you so as to help you continue to grow in your walk with Jesus. Covering you in prayer, my son!

Walk In A Manner Worthy

Darrin's Story

Because of stories like the one you are about to read, I never argue when someone says "God works in mysterious ways." I had no idea what was coming when I stopped at a friend's place of business to pick up something he wanted to give me. Andy had sent me a Google map link to get there, but somehow I passed by the place I was supposed to go to be where I was "supposed" to be, at least from God's perspective.

I didn't have much time for this particular errand as I was headed to a meeting 30 miles south and I was already running a tad late. After parking my car, I wandered in a big warehouse that smelled of cut wood, ready to be used in Andy's construction business. There appeared to be no one around and I thus assumed people had gone out for lunch. Nonetheless, I continued to wander the premises in case there was indeed someone in an area I had not yet explored.

Upon opening a door, leading where I didn't know, I saw a 50-ish man washing out a bucket. He didn't see me, so I cleared my throat so as not to startle him should he turn around and see an unexpected guest in his proximity. I proceeded to ask him if Andy was around. He pointed out the window and let me know that if he was available, he'd be in the building down the road a bit. I thanked him and started for the door.

Just as I was shutting it behind me, I heard him ask my name. I wondered why it mattered to him, but being the gregarious individual that I am, I told him. His face lit up. He replied, "I thought so. I'm Darrin (last name). Do you remember me? You look the same as you did almost 40 years ago."

My heart raced. I couldn't believe my ears. Was this man really the grown up version of one of my favorite kids back when I worked as a residential counselor in a treatment facility back in the early 80's? Tears welled as he continued to remind me of me in past days, as that zealous 23-year-old young man who wanted to save the world.

I told Darrin that I had seen his name on a newscast a couple years ago and did my best to try to find him, wondering if that man on the news was indeed the same person I had known years earlier. He affirmed with a chuckle that, yes, it was him and it was because he had done a good thing, the word *good* being emphasized. He and a buddy had witnessed a man beating a lady with a hammer and stepped in to

Darrin's Story

save her from being murdered. Darrin beamed as he shared that piece of his life.

Because I had to get to my scheduled meeting, I asked Darrin if we could do lunch sometime soon to which he readily agreed. I later got his cell number from Andy and texted him right away. I was very much looking forward to catching up after four decades and, as I typically do, I prayed that God would open doors for me to talk to Darrin about my faith. I was pretty certain that particular prayer would be answered in the affirmative since it was obviously God's divine appointment that I met Darrin in this most unexpected way. I have learned over the years of following Jesus that there are no "coincidences" in the Christian realm.

A week passed and our scheduled appointment for lunch finally arrived. I had so many questions for him. Would he be willing to share his life to the degree I was interested? I soon found that the answer was a resounding "yes." Darrin was primed to share his life and also to hear about mine. He brought back many memories from what seemed like eons ago. He shared with me his family dysfunction that initiated his placement at Beloit and the number of places he had been both before and after said placement.

Darrin reported that he intuitively knew the employees at this facility who were there because it was for them just a job or because they really cared about the kids that were placed. He emphatically stated he knew I was there because I cared about helping people. I knew for myself that this statement was true, but was delighted to know he believed it also. Darrin blew me away with information about me that I cannot imagine holding onto for 40 years. He knew my FULL NAME and where I went to college. Too, he wondered, as have I, about the other residents that he had earlier named, how they were faring in life. He asked me about my colleague counselors, most of whom were on my list of Facebook friends. Darrin did not do social media although he had contemplated starting a page just so he could check up on those he remembered.

Sadness permeated his stories of trauma, grief and loss. He had been married twice. His first wife died, subsequently leaving their children with her parents who then turned his children against him. Admittedly his choices originated their distrust of him. He took full responsibility but the ongoing sadness was visible in his eyes. His second wife was "crazy" as he described her. Their children were no longer in his life either. More grief. Jail, prison, bondage to drugs and alcohol, divorce, homelessness – all taking their toll on him emotionally and physically, to the point of eventually having a stroke that left him in a mental stupor most days. His medications had helped the mental and emotional fog, but yet his life was not how he had dreamed back when he was 14 and had me in his life.

He reported that he had spent a year in a faith-based mission program where, for the first time, he was challenged about his own parents having wounds that hindered them from loving him the way he longed to be loved as a little boy. Both his parents had poor parenting growing up, thus they, too, tried to mask their pain with bad choices, leaving Little Darrin vulnerable and alone. He was told so often that he was a "bad kid" that he believed it and lived accordingly. He had grown so tired of trying to earn love that he succumbed to giving up, rebelling against societal norms and mores. He started looking for love in all the wrong places and paid a great price in so doing.

As he shared one sad event after another my heart felt overwhelming compassion for him. He was a physically and emotionally spent man. The only real joy he could recount was being hired by my friend, Andy, whom Darrin conveyed believed in him even more than he believed in himself. Andy employed Darrin two years prior and had treated him well, helping him both financially and also by assigning him jobs that he could perform given his stroke disabilities. If Darrin couldn't do one job, Andy found another one where he could find success. This was a great blessing to Darrin who was trying hard to get his life together in the midst of all the tribulation he had just described in depressed detail. It was at this point I felt prompted to remind him of my Christian beliefs, something he had remembered me possessing years ago. It was time to walk through the door God had just opened for me.

The grace to tell this broken man about my Father's love was palpable to me. I seemed to feel for Darrin the love that Christ had for him and I was anxious to reflect to him that same love. Darrin remembered my sharing my Christian testimony (which can be read it at the end of this book) years ago. He believed in God but did not understand the concept of repentance, forgiveness and identity of being what Scripture calls a "new creation" – when Jesus forgives and robes His children in His own righteousness.

Darrin acknowledged he had many sins. He acknowledged that he believed that Jesus came to die on the cross, shedding His blood to forgive all sins. He seemed to understand that concept for the sake of others but had a hard time, as we all do, grasping it for himself. I shared with him that Jesus wasn't looking for perfection as He already knew Darrin was broken and hurting. Trying to clean ourselves up, I told him, was analogous to trying to stop all bleeding before going to the ER. I reminded

Darrin's Story

him, too, that God knew all the hurdles in his life and why it was hard for him to trust and step out in faith. Yet, that is exactly what Darrin did as he humbled himself before God and me, by praying out loud for forgiveness and asking God to make him a new man. There was no fanfare, no angels, no audible voices. Just one man's jump of faith into the arms of what he believed was a forgiving and loving God who could give him a peace and joy in the midst of his sorrow and pain.

Time will tell what God will do in and through this man for whom He had given me a heart of love decades ago. Darrin allowed me to take a picture of us together before departing. Interestingly, when I posted this picture of us on Facebook with a brief synopsis of what happened during our time together, I got more responses and comments than I remember getting for anything I have ever posted in the many years I've had a FB account. To date, over 430 friends have hit the like/heart symbol acknowledging the incredulity of this story. Comments came from those who praised God with me for astonishingly connecting dots over the years culminating in a lost sheep coming to the Good Shepherd. Many indicated they shed happy tears as they read the short post with the corresponding snapshot of Darrin and me.

I will never understand the ways of the God whom I serve. Sowing seeds, later reaping a harvest. As I entrust myself to Him, I more clearly see His hand mightily at work to bring redemption to a hurting and dying world - to those in bondage to sin and to the emotional consequences of it. I am honored to have been used in Darrin's life and grateful that he wants to maintain a friendship now that we've reconnected after so many years. He covets the encouragement and love from me (and others) that he received from me in his most vulnerable early years, something that he fondly cherished even in the absence of personal relationship until the present.

Darrin texted me shortly after our lunch meeting, out of the blue. He wrote "GOD is LOVE. Those who do not know God do not know love. I am forever grateful to you for showing me love. Then and now. Thank you."

He can now start looking for love in all the right places.

Walk In A Manner Worthy

I had asked James, my former foster son, to write a blurb to coincide with an article I wrote for FOSTERING FAMILIES TODAY magazine. He agreed to do so. Imagine my astonishment when he wanted to read to me over the phone his "blurb". I had no idea he was such a talented writer of prose although I had knowledge of his artistry and poem writing. The following two articles were published in the same issue of FFT giving two distinct perspectives of identical situations. Thank you, James Michael Nieman, for your contribution to not only my book, but to my life.

Combez Inn

I had just found out that I wasn't going home and was going to a stupid foster home instead. Great!!! I'd been locked up in state homes for about 4 years or so. I'd been on probation, in and out of programs for delinquents, and gone through many suspensions/expulsions from public schools. I wasn't a kid everyone would want. Fights, gang-banger background, stealing cars, petty theft, running away from home and extensive drug use. I was a poster child for "Bad Boys".

This abridged story begins in 1996 just before I turned 16. I was court-ordered into "Children's Square USA" in Council Bluffs, Iowa. This program was a last resort before being incarcerated in the state training school until I was 18. This was the first institution in which I'd been placed that made a difference in my life. The others were very strict and mean. It was for a purpose though – to scare a person straight. It didn't work. I became more "hardcore" and built an even stronger wall of hatred around my heart. My probation officer finally sent me to a facility that specialized in teamwork, competitiveness, leadership, family environment, etc. I had someone listen to me rather than pushing me away as if I were a rabid dog.

I was able to work my way back into society. I earned my privileges to go to public school and go outside unsupervised to shoot some hoop or walk around. That may not sound like a big deal to most people, but after being locked up in 6 x 8 cells wearing a jumpsuit, having to look down all day, responding "yes sir, no ma'am" to everything said and done, having one minute to do "number one" and two minutes to do "number two", 4 minutes to both brush teeth and shower, sit facing the wall for 4 hours at a time without moving, and getting yelled at constantly - walking alone and going to school was a treasure!

Towards the end of my stay at Children's' Square, I had been informed that I was going to a foster home instead of HOME! I was quite upset as I had been under the

Combez Inn

impression that I was going through all this CRAP (best word to describe how I felt w/out actually cussing) to return home only to find out I was deceived! I was scheduled the following weekend to do an "introductory visit" to a Mr. Kim Combes' home to get a feel of what I was getting into. Not thrilled!

I talked with Kim on the phone before I went to his home that weekend and he seemed like a nice guy, yet I still wasn't thrilled about the situation. Oh well... I had to do it. The alternatives were even less appealing.

After being transported from Council Bluffs, I waited in the probation office to meet the man who was to be in charge of yet another adventure in my life. After sitting awhile, in walks a man with a cheerful jump in his walk. This did not seem normal!!!! He had a goatee, graying hair, big glasses and a hat that he wore with the bill high on his head (something that was considered "cool" to do in the 80's) revealing his bangs. "Great!!" I thought as he walked by me. I secretly hoped this "dork" wasn't Kim.

After a few minutes, my probation officer introduced me to Kim Combes. It WAS him! I had just become even less thrilled.

I grabbed the bag I had packed for the weekend and followed him to his car. I was nervous and a little scared, but gave no hint to feeling that way. I was too cool and hardcore for that. We "small talked" to get to know each other a little better on the ride to his home. Once there, he showed me the room in which I would be staying and introduced me to my new "FBs" (foster brothers).

It wasn't as bad as I thought. Kim was a very kind man and offered all he had to me in the first few moments of meeting him. This seemed very unusual to me! Does this guy realize my background? Is he sure he wants to do this? I could take total advantage of this guy! I couldn't help but think like a criminal... I was a criminal! This man had just offered me a home and everything in it. Yet, I still couldn't help but think of ways to rip him off and in other ways get into trouble.

Interestingly, I did not rip him off. In the wall of hatred around my heart there were still a few bricks missing. This allowed my compassion and conscience to still be shown and, strangely, some of my hardcore shell melted which allowed me to confide in this new, strange man in my life.

Kim and I talked non-stop getting to know each other a lot better. While on this pre-placement visit, we stayed up watching TV and I felt comfortable enough to sit close to him as he talked. Per my request, he massaged my neck, releasing some of the anger and tension I had built up inside. It was during these talks that I discovered that Kim was a Christian. A "hard core Bible-banger" is what I had called it. Now it started making sense to me! This is why he treats me this way! God is helping him to deal with guys like me! Kim was trying to guide me by showing me kindness. Weird! This was definitely a new experience. It was so comfortable, that I made it quite uncomfortable. Closeness scared me. A lot! It was foreign to me.

The weekend visit was great! I was actually glad to meet the man with an unusual happy bounce in his walk. I thanked him for the weekend and went back to Children's Square.

When I got back I was told that I was going to live in Kim's home. I finished my stay at Children's Square and graduated the program that week. The following weekend I moved into Kim's home permanently. I say permanently for a good reason. Little did I know at the time that Kim's would become a permanent safe haven for me. I still consider Kim's to be home today. My own personal, comfortable getaway. The "Combez Inn" (his nickname was Bez growing up so I occasionally refer to him as Comb-Bez, making his one syllable last name, two). This was the beginning of a new chapter in my life...a long, difficult and fun chapter.

The first week went rather well. Kim and I started a nightly routine of watching "Mad About You" and the "Untouchables" on TV. Kind of ironic, really. Mad and untouchable. What a great combination!! (sarcasm).

Kim lived in a college town, Ames Iowa. I enrolled at Ames High School and did well. I, of course, had my problems with authority, but that was to be expected of me. I hated authority. I got into my fair share of fights and trouble at school. Even had my moments with Kim. Not a shocker...not yet anyway.

When I moved into Kim's home, he was in the process of moving into a bigger house so all of us FBs would have more room. Turns out the home that was found was in Podunk, IA...a small town called Colo. Just great!!! Street-wise kids in a small, judgmental, racist town. How wonderful!!! We all went through a hard transition.

It seemed the whole town, excluding a small few, talked horribly of us. How Kim held it together I don't know. We were considered the trash of the town. The people in Colo treated my FBs and me very rudely.

Combez Inn

Now don't get me wrong, the FBs and I did our fair share of terrorizing. Rebels! Big time! We (I) put Kim through hell, on top of everything else. How he maintained through all of this I don't fully understand, but I do know it was because of God's help, Kim's prayers, and his love for us.

Everywhere I lived or was placed, I became some sort of a leader for my peers. People looked up to me no matter how bad or good my example. This caused a lot of problems. I was always a ringleader and people followed, even if I didn't want them to! Kim knew this very well and watched my effects on everyone around me. No matter how much of a jerk I was to people, they still wanted to be around me and do what I was doing. Not good!

I was selling beer/liquor out of Kim's garage, selling cigarettes to my FBs and other neighborhood kids, and occasionally selling drugs. Unknowingly to him, Kim would hang out with me and/or my FBs while we were getting more and more intoxicated with each word spoke as we spiked the fruit juice that he provided for us. Not until later did he find out about my actions. I (and another brother) even trapped one of the FBs in a cubbyhole in the garage and threw fiery newspapers at him! I made obscene comments and gestures toward Kim on many occasions. One that I vividly remember happened on a hot, sticky summer night.

Some of my brothers and I were upstairs wearing only our boxers trying to stay cool (the AC was broken) and irritating Kim by not settling down to sleep. There was a disagreement between Kim and me. I, in defiance, being the hard head I was, I grabbed my crotch, pulled up, and told Kim I thought he was being very cocky, accenting both syllables of the word for emphasis. That was very rude of me and he was furious! Hence the reason I did it. I did a lot of things to irritate him.

My temper was a big issue too. I told Kim at one point "if it wasn't for laws you'd be dead!" I meant it! My anger was no laughing matter! I had assaulted a lot of people including adults. I was no wimp! I was physically well built and grew up fighting. It was second nature to me. In one argument, I had even thrown his patio table out into the yard! At midnight!! I was a real jerk!

One evening things had gotten so out of control that Kim hit his breaking point. We had all beaten Kim's wall of strength down to a pile of rubble and despair. I had accomplished my unwritten goal of anger and hatred...break down the people who cared most for me. I was a jackass. Kim stated he quit and that the next day he was going to turn in his foster care license. We were to be placed elsewhere. For the other guys, that meant other foster homes. For me, it most likely meant the training school.

He was not joking. This man had done everything in his power for us. All we could do to pay him back was figuratively spit in his face. It was at this point my heart felt like a glass being thrust to the floor, shattering into shards of sharp despair. I had screwed up bad. Kim loved me and I didn't love him back. It wasn't fair. This brave Christian man felt at a loss with us, with himself, and with God. I felt horrible. While the other foster boys talked and whispered about where they would go, I humbly asked my foster father to go on a walk with me.

After a short time, we arrived at the park in the center of town and sat at a picnic table. This was a very uncomfortable moment for me. Tears began to fall down my face. This was very unusual for me to do. I literally had not cried since I was a little boy. My heart had so hardened over the years that emotions were erased from my normal behavior.

As the tears fell, in a weakened, sobbing voice, I told Kim, "I have nowhere to go." I was being sincere. I asked him not to quit because I needed him. He had been more of a father to me in the short time I had been with him than my own dad had. (That's how I felt at that time in my life. I've gained more respect and have more love for my biological father now than I had then. That, too, is another story.)

To sum up our walk to the park, we hugged while in tears and broken down. If I remember correctly, I think Kim prayed for the both of us while we sat at that picnic table in the middle of a dark park with only the moon to illuminate our faces of sadness, which also now reflected hope for the future. Kim didn't give up on me and I got to stay in his home.

There were many more hard times, but I tried to improve myself. I even volunteered my time to Habitat for Humanity in town to better our household name. I wanted the people of Colo and surrounding areas to see that Kim was a good man and was making better people out of us "bad boys." Long story short, it worked! People started liking us! I was doing well in school! I was a starter on the Varsity football team and people that made fun of me/disliked me, became my friends. This had a lot to do with my foster dad's guidance.

Kim wasn't married when I lived with him. He got married to Diane in April 1999, less than a year after I left his home. At first, it was really weird to see him with a wife and daughter, but I got used to it after some time. I was honored to be

Combez Inn

head usher at his wedding and even got teary as I hugged him and Diane after the ceremony. Since then, I've had my ups and downs. I've been in and out of lock up a few times as an adult and had problems with drug addictions, but I have always had Kim by my side through it all.

I hope all kids who go through foster care can have a relationship with their foster parents the way I do. I am very close with them to this day and believe I always will be. Kim and Diane have challenged me to become closer to God and have given me another family. I've had several foster brothers but none of those relationships compare to the one I have with my sister, Nikki, and little brother, James Logan, who was named after me.

I love Diane and her daughter, Nikki, very much. They have accepted me and love me as well! It is a good feeling! James Logan, who they adopted after being married, also loves me as I do him! They are currently fostering a sibling group of four, ranging in age from 12 to 6. These kids now have a place in my heart as well. It's great! I can't describe the love that this family has! I wouldn't even know it myself if it weren't for a man named Kim Combes and a program called foster care.

You've just finished James' point of view, now welcome to mine:

I was livid. How dare he be so disrespectful – and in front of the other teen boys I had living in my home also. It was difficult enough to foster obstreperous older adolescents as a single parent, but with the stress of just moving to a small, sleepy town that did not understand, nor appreciate my Christian ministry, I was always only moments away from retiring my foster care license. This was one of those moments. I began longing for the return of a sane life not filled with total chaos caused by housemates that seemed concerned only for themselves.

James was almost 17, a very bright, but rebellious young man. Life had dealt him some bad cards but instead of playing fairly with what he had, he chose to draw from the deck some that worsened his playing position. Landing in my home was one of his last chances before spending the rest of his minor years in the State Training School. I saw in him much potential for making a positive impact on society and being successful in whatever constructive endeavor he would choose for himself. However, when his anger and rage reared their ugly heads, darkness clouded my positive outlook on his future life.

Just weeks before, "Mr. Attitude" hurled our metal patio table off the porch onto the front lawn while assaulting me with his vulgarities about a decision I had just made. The fact it was after midnight on an otherwise very quiet night gave me the shivers thinking about how many neighbors may soon be calling the local sheriff's office. Too, I believed that his rage would block his cognitive reasoning enough to forget the threat of potential future consequences should he decide to be physically aggressive towards his foster parent. After all, it wasn't like he hadn't been assaultive to other adults in the past. I prayed that my anger de-escalation skills would save me from a beating that I would not soon forget (he later verbalized to me that if it weren't for laws, I'd have been dead as anger towards me bolted through him). Coming from a "gangbanger" background, his fists knew confrontation and the picture was bleak for those confronted.

I tried to keep my voice calm and quiet as his 13 year old brother, Matthew, watched yet another explosive incident involving his older sibling and an authority figure. In less than 15 minutes James began to soften. His rage dissipated giving way to a despairing appearance, all color drained from his face. Difficult as it was for him, he apologized and submitted to the decision I had earlier made. He soon escaped with the Sandman to his sleep retreat where exhaustion, both physical and emotional, overtook him.

But now, standing in James' room a half-hour past their bedtime, all four of my charges dressed only in their boxer shorts, appeared ready to rumble. I was emotionally exhausted from the last two months of trying to adjust to our new home and hearing uninformed, if not ill-intentioned, comments coming from the townspeople. The heat of the summer without a working central air system coupled with the obnoxious, rambunctious behaviors of four boys who did not like moving from a university town to Podunk, Iowa was starting to push me over the top.

I was beginning to regret trying to relive my teen years in a small Northwest Iowa town where I grew up. Something inside of me had yearned for the less expensive, more neighborly environment of small town living. So far, with the exception of a few, it wasn't very friendly. A handful of people reached out and seemed willing to give the boys and me a fair chance to prove ourselves, but still I missed the support of my friends in Ames only 20 miles away. In any event, the responsibility of four youth who apparently could "give a damn about anything" was eating away at me. My patience and tolerance for disrespect towards me, my possessions, my beliefs and value system were wearing precariously thin.

With controlled anger and deliberate disrespect, James cupped his groin and

Combez Inn

lifted his genitals towards his belly, and told me with drawn-out syllables, that in his opinion, I was getting pretty "cock-key" with my attitude. Laughter erupted throughout the room as I felt the heat of anger, defeat, discouragement, and humiliation surge through my body. With nothing constructive to say, I retreated while boisterous jocularity echoed behind me, trailing me down the old wooden staircase in my turn-of-the-century home. I could only image the illustrative adjectives describing my character rolling off the tongues of the brood of vipers all gathered just one floor above me. I once more contemplated giving up on ever making a dent in their anger-coated armor surrounding the marshmallow hearts longing to be loved, nurtured and accepted unconditionally. Sleep evaded me this night as my brain and viscera were tortured with weighing the ramifications of tossing in the towel against the emotional turmoil I would surely endure if I didn't.

Finding several 40 ounce bottles of beer in my garage was the final straw. Just four nights before, I discovered the aforementioned brood had been drinking spiked grapefruit drink in one of the four bedrooms. To top it off, before I figured it out, I had been with them casually discussing the events of the day. I was totally oblivious to the fact they were getting closer to being drunk with every word we spoke. It was demanding trying to keep on top of the games played by young men from backgrounds that invited the honing of their conniving skills. I was being paid by the State to do therapeutic interventions with these difficult to place schemers. In my humble estimation, I was failing miserably. Finding the beer was yet another painful slap to my already battered and bruised social worker/foster parent ego.

"I quit, guys. You win", I told them on this fateful Thursday night. "I'm calling DHS tomorrow to ask them to find homes for all of you before Tuesday. I can't take this anymore. You want to pull your crap, not work on your issues...take it somewhere else", I droned pathetically. The fun-loving, exuberant, optimist I thought I was, was gone. I had been taking difficult teens for three years and I no longer had the internal fortitude to continue. My affect and voice reflected the apathy that flooded every fiber of my being. In four days, my foster parenting career would be ended. Even with this light at the end of the tunnel, depression clung like a wet blanket to my soul.

"Brad" picked up the phone to call our private agency worker, the friend who licensed me 3 years earlier. He and I both knew that "Donna" would not care that it was midnight. She liked us and had always been supportive of me and my household. While Brad spoke with our worker, the only woman he had ever trusted, James asked if we could go for a walk. The other two spoke in whispers, probably discussing where they would be living as of the next week.

The town park was where we arrived as James, placed with me only 3½ months, dropped his walls to expose some vulnerability. "Kim," he said tearfully, "I have nowhere else to go. You can't give up your license." He choked on his words as the tears flowed more readily. "You have been closer to me as a parent than both my parents put together."

Now whether that last statement was true is debatable. The fact that wasn't debatable, however, was that on his good days we got along very well. Only my first placement – Eddie, for whom I had become a foster parent – was as easy for me to talk with as James. James and I had both experienced similar things growing up, giving us a commonality on which to base a good friendship once my parenting days of him ceased. Until then, I would continue to be the parent that I was contracted to be.

Many people use tears as a manipulative tool. James' personality was not such that he would stoop to crying to gain what he wanted. On the contrary, crying was almost as foreign to him as engaging in lively Latin discourse. He trained himself well to endure pain, both physical and emotional. His tears were real. Hope once more rose within me, against all odds.

It has been three years since James entered my life. In that time, the community has more readily accepted my family and ministry. James helped that to happen by volunteering his time and talent in a Habitat for Humanity project in town. He also won accolades on the football field his first fall in this school district, having fought the "bad foster kid" reputation he was given before anyone really got to know him. He was "student of the month" several times – his picture hanging in the school hallway in recognition. His artwork and poetry showed much aptitude…along with the confusion and pain swimming inside his heart and soul. Drugs are no longer a part of his life. Still, not all of his decisions have been wise or good, but yet he has many outstanding qualities if one would only look past the hard-core exterior fabricated to protect the vulnerable facets of his personality and character.

James left my home in July 1998 just prior to his 18th birthday. He was an usher at my wedding a year ago. He got teary as he hugged us after I spun my bride around following being pronounced man and wife. He adores our 11 year old daughter (and vice versa). He has been up and down, in jail and out of jail, doing well, not doing well, back to doing well. He has spent many a night sleeping on our couch. We have

Combez Inn

logged many more hours of conversation. Through it all, a bond remains. Our year old adoptive son bears his name. For his 19th birthday James wanted us to adopt him, even after a heavy-duty conflict with us just a couple weeks before. We could not legally, of course, do this. At his suggestion, however, using my best "legal-ese", I drew up a certificate on my PC. It is signed by me, my wife, and James - nicely framed, and setting in my office - again, all at James' request.

Last summer, while relaxing on the wrought iron gliding porch swing Diane and I bought with wedding money, James, never really being verbally demonstrative with affection, surprised and honored me with the following: "Kim, what I am about to say, I may never say again and I don't want you to sh-- a brick when I say this now. You and Matthew are my best friends and I love you." No influence from drugs or alcohol...just speaking frankly from his heart.

Am I glad I went for that midnight walk with James to the park three summers ago? Am I glad I did not resign as a foster parent that night? Yes...a resounding YES! We know we have impacted the life of at least one young man. By God's grace and with His strength, Diane and I will continue to do so - one life at a time, one day at a time.

Self-Injurious Behavior: A Cutter's Story

This author asked James to write on the topic of self-injurious behaviors. These articles, one written by James and the other by me (next in line) were published in FFT simultaneously. It is my desire that both of articles will be not only educational, but of great benefit to any reader who may have in their circle an individual who wrestles with this coping mechanism.

I'm alone in my room and I hate myself. The lights are dim, the TV is on, and the music is playing on the stereo just barely loud enough to make it out. Inside my heart I can't decide how I feel or if I feel anything at all.

So I stare at... then playfully glide... the blade of my knife across my open clammy, luke-warm hands. Now that the blade softly runs across my fingers I get the urge... I get the desire to feel something because I can't feel anything. I can't feel angry or sad or happy...nothing. Just me and a dark emptiness all around me... and a burning inside.

I touch the blade to my stomach. I press it against my skin with great pressure; I can feel the steel break the first layer of skin. I push even harder. Now I can see a little blood appear on each side of the knife. But still I feel nothing. I push even harder and pull it across my flesh fast, hard and without care! I let out a small grunt of satisfaction. Now I can feel something! The laceration is deep and has opened itself almost a finger's width when stretched out. I can feel the subtle tickle of my blood as it slowly and thickly flows down across my skin. I touch it, then smear it all over my quivering abs. I feel alone, but I don't cry. I shut myself off and wait. For what I'm not sure, but I wait.

It is apparent I have struggled with self-injurious behavior. I'm not going to tell you anything out of a book or even try to make sense of why people do this to themselves

I can speak only for myself as to why I struggled with my addiction to injure and scar my body. My guess is that most people who self-injure have similar thoughts and reasons for their choice of actions. Personally, I don't have one specific reason for why I do it. I have several.

For now, forget about what books, trainers, and doctors have said, taught or expressed to you as they probably don't know from personal experience, but from

Self-Injurious Behaviors: A Cutter's Story

educated guesses and theories. They are trying to understand and have some good insight, but not all is accurate. It's pretty much impossible to get accurate on this subject as even the subject performing these acts on self can't make perfect sense of their behavior. To further explain, I'll give some reasons why I chose (and still sometimes choose) to do this to myself.

So...here we go. So many times I have chosen to cut, burn and/or hit myself repeatedly for such reasons as wanting some sort of sympathy or attention. I would cut my arms and stomach so people could see the wounds if I desired them to or I could hide them with a shirt if I wanted to conceal them.

I cut myself because I felt empty inside or a desire to see how badly I could injure myself without actually committing suicide. It's so hard to explain reasons why! I sometimes don't have a solid reason for the act. "Hurting" myself by burning, cutting and hitting doesn't really "hurt" at all but actually gives me pleasure and relief.

It is a way to feel alive while wanting to die. I didn't always want to die when performing these acts on myself. So this isn't always a hint for wanting to commit suicide. The want for ending ones own life depends on the emotion. Usually the want to commit suicide comes from severe depression and anxiety. It comes from overwhelming circumstances and stress and confusion. Common sense and rational thought are blocked by extreme emotion – suicide thus becomes the most attractive and easy solution to ending the pain and brokenness in one's heart.

Without the release of self-injurious behavior, I believe that suicide numbers would increase. "Hurting" myself would give me temporary pleasure and help me to release the bottled and swallowed pain inside my heart. Without the option of wounding myself to feel better suicide would become more and more attractive for my escape from this strange unsettling "dream" of life.

Self-injurious behavior comes from many circumstances in a person's life. Mine is because of physical/sexual/emotional abuse as well as drug abuse. In the act of being physically abused I would get punched in the face. It would leave a mark or a bruise (I tried numerous times to inform people that I was being abused but no one would believe me!). I didn't think the wound my offender left was big or visible enough. Thus, I would punch myself and bang my head against a wall repeatedly to make the wound bigger and more visible. I believed that someone would finally believe me. Sometimes it was almost orgasmic to injure myself.

Walk In A Manner Worthy

Being abused physically, emotionally and sexually made me doubt my self-worth. I felt like no one cared so what difference did it make what I did to myself. Being subjected to pain throughout my life created an addiction to it. So if it weren't another "hurting" me, I would do it to myself as it actually seemed to improve my self-esteem.

Drug abuse was also a gateway to this behavior. Not only is using drugs self-injurious, it becomes a math problem with a bad outcome. Using drugs + self-injurious behaviors (cutting/hitting/burning) = extreme danger! Under the influence of narcotics I was much more prone to hurt myself since my body was already numb from the drugs. I thus would make bigger and deeper injuries on my body.

I really don't know how to make sense of this behavior, but I hope I gave some idea of why self-injurious behavior occurs. There are unlimited possibilities as to why someone would do this, including simple boredom.

Self-injurious behavior is dangerous and an addiction. The only way anyone can help the subject is to be open, listen, and show concern without using force or telling him/her they can't do it anymore. It is up to the subject to stop or minimize this behavior. I believe the best way to conquer this addition is to pray and seek help and strength from God.

Self-Injurious Behaviors: Help Stop The Pain

His pacing continued, much like a caged, angry lion. He was struggling... seemingly having no way of verbalizing the pent up emotion swirling destructively inside him. He was about to burst; something had to give. Diane and I were helpless to alleviate his pain. We escaped into Fear Factor playing on TV, not realizing that we were about to experience our own "fear factor" momentarily.

James (our 24- year-old former foster son) went to the kitchen. Within seconds we heard sounds orgasmic in nature. Baffled, we waited what seemed like an eternity. He emerged from the kitchen, calm...relieved from the stress he was demonstrating just moments before. We pursued him as he sat reticent at the dining table. Diane questioned him. No response. Thinking he would talk if it were just the two of us, Diane left the room. Initially evasive to my interrogation, he finally asked me "Do you really want to know?" As I nodded yes, he lifted his shirt revealing a 1-2 inch bloody wound, a manifestation of his solution to the overwhelming negative feelings now pacified. As a surgeon skillfully removes a malignant tumor, James had successfully (for the moment anyway) removed the cancer of unbearable pain with one swipe of a blade.

Self-injurious behavior! This phenomenon, recently labeled the "anorexia of the new millennium", is an ever-growing epidemic amongst our youth culture today, but is not exclusive to teens only. A nationwide study conducted in 2002 found that one out of every 200 teen girls regularly harms herself. About 72% say they cut themselves; others burn themselves, hit themselves and even break their own bones. Seventy-eight percent use a combination of methods of self-injury. Males, too, utilize self-harm to relieve the pain and emptiness they experience internally.

Not to be confused with ritual bodily harm as graphically portrayed in the 1970"s film "A Man Called Horse", current self-injurious behaviors (SIB) are the manifestations of deeper underlying problems unable to be verbalized by those experiencing incredible inner turmoil. The cuts, burns and broken bones are simply the visible expressions of internal hopelessness and despair. Cutting may be a way to express on the skin what is difficult to express under the skin.

There is no paucity of literature regarding SIB. Google indicated well over 9 million links to be explored under this heading. The surfer is directed to "definitions of, causes, and treatments for" this enigmatic behavior now being discussed in myriad counseling offices and familial homes where desperate loved ones are trying to sort out their own confused, horrified emotions associated with SIB.

Walk In A Manner Worthy

To clarify, self-injurious behavior does not fall, by definition, under any behaviors done as a rite of passage (i.e. Native American Sun Vows), for bodily ornamentation (tattoos, belly rings, etc.), for sexual pleasure (masochism), or purely for emotional manipulation of authority figures (to "get back" at parents) although this might be a "fringe benefit." Most researchers agree that self-injury is self-inflicted physical harm severe enough to cause tissue damage or marks that last for several hours or permanently, done without suicidal intent. While cutting is the most universal type of SIB, head-banging and burning are also viable methods for self-injurers.

An acquaintance of mine started his self-injury when he accidentally slammed his fingers in a car door while struggling with suicidal ideations. The intensity of physical pain superseded the emotional intensity, thus the genesis of his self-inflicted harm. Other forms of SIB include skin-picking, hair pulling, hitting objects with the body or vice versa. One man in his 20's admitted that he had purposely broken the bones in his feet many times by dropping 5 lb grocery cans on them. The combination of pain/pleasure is euphoric, thus addictive in nature.

It works like this. The tension and stress of life build. Negative, self-derogatory thoughts condemn. Emotions escalate to dangerously high levels, to the extent an injurer believes it cannot be endured. A release is needed. Dissociation, then the injury. Endorphins in the body are released. Euphoria. Emotions de-escalate. Stabilization. Shame and guilt for behaviors surface. Tension mounts. Negative thoughts condemn...... The cycle continues.

It is erroneously assumed that SIB is a precursor to suicide, thus it must be stopped to deter inevitable death. Those who work with cutters challenge this conventional thinking. Perhaps cutting is a way to stop a young person from becoming yet another statistic. Imagine, then, that the razor, the glass, the nail...is the injurer's "social support". Remove it and one takes away the motivation to stay alive. Doctors can occasionally glean from the look of the wound whether suicidal intent may be present. Self-injurers will have many wounds in various degrees of healing while a suicidal patient may have no visible indications of a self-injurious history.

It's very difficult to wrap one's mind around this concept. CUTTING IS A WAY TO STAY ALIVE?!? In speaking with James verification was indeed given that, yes, chances of a successful suicide would likely increase if the self-injurious behaviors weren't an option. The pain/euphoria cycle may very well be the act that keeps injurers from eventual demise.

Cajoling, threats and ultimatums are useless for getting individuals to cease and

Self-Injurious Behaviors: Help Stop The Pain

desist with the SIB. In fact, these will likely increase the desire for release in a self-violent way. One may feel more and more isolated from those that love them as it isn't "safe" to share their shameful secret. Persons who are taken to psychiatric wards by frightened caregivers are hindered, not helped, by this act. While hospital rooms are void of hurtful objects, those who have an overwhelming urge to cut will utilize anything. Many cutters have admitted to biting/scratching themselves, pouring in the wound the salt that comes with their meals, then pressing against the wound the ice that comes in the drink cup. This 3-step action will create a wound similar to that of a fire burn with the same painful/euphoric effect. Too, to take away the usual items of self-harm, the self-injurer may have to resort to something that will leave far more damage than the razor to get the same euphoric effect.

The term "self-mutilation" is one associated with SIB. However, self-injurers do not appreciate this idiom, as it seems to reflect "intent". While SIB does leave marks/scars, this is a secondary characteristic, not one that deliberate so as to show off battle scars. Many that self-harm will wear clothing that hides the proof of their choice, such as long-sleeve shirts and pants even on stifling, hot summer days.

If SIB is a manifestation of presenting problems, what might be the actual problems? Self-injurers have reported using SIB to maintain a sense of security or feelings of uniqueness (I'll hurt me before I let you hurt me). They feel alienated by family and friends with no sense of validation for who they are. Sexual abuse victims who self-harm believe they need to be "punished" for what happened to them, thus they utilize cutting or other methods. Some use SIB to divert attention (inner or outer) from issues too painful to examine. Others feel "nothing". Self-injury and the resulting pain/blood reminds the individual that they are indeed still in the land of the living. SIB is sometimes the result of catastrophic losses in childhood, too overwhelming to deal with. Generally, however, relationships are the cause of SIB and thus relationships are the antidote.

Andrew Levander, Clinical Director of Vista Del Mar in Southern California writes:

> "Many therapeutic approaches have been and are being developed to help self-harmers learn new coping mechanisms and teach them how to use those techniques instead of self-injury. This does not mean that patients should be coerced into stopping self-injury. Any attempts to reduce or control the amount of self-harm a person does should be based in the client's willingness to undertake the difficult work of controlling and/or

stopping self-injury. Treatment should not be based on a practitioner's personal feelings about the practice of self-harm."

Non-medical caregivers can be a part of the healing process if their own emotions/actions are handled in a loving, non-threatening way. Reading this article is the start of helping a loved one through the pain of SIB. Continue to read books and resources (remember to GOOGLE for a plethora of information). If a self-injurer wants to talk, focus on the underlying issues, not the behaviors. Accept how you feel about self-harm and realize that you may need your own support group to help another. Show that you are a safe person to talk with, but don't push a person to do so. Listen, but show an interest by asking questions in a non-judgmental way. Help to work out triggers to self-harm and how a self-harmer can find distractions instead of using razors, etc. Encourage a self-injurer to start a diary where they can write down how they are feeling and take notes of when, how, and why they self-harm.

Do not ignore the self-injurer. Treat them as you usually would. Be respectful and understanding. Shouting and "freaking out" are not beneficial for anyone. To say "snap out of it" or "you're crazy for cutting" is detrimental to the relationship you want to create. As hard as it is, do not take it personally. It's not about you, but about what a self-injurer cannot yet express in healthy ways. Stay "one down" by stating you don't understand, but that you want to. Ask "How would you like me to respond to this?" Do not use "emotional blackmail" to get the behaviors to stop. This will instill more guilt and thus the desire to do harm again. When you discover a self-injurer in the act, stay calm. Do what you would do if they would have fallen down and scraped a knee...nurture them (this will not reinforce the behavior, but will develop the trust between you and the self-harmer). Tell them you love them. Then tell them again.

Self-injurers often find the urge to hurt themselves uncontrollable. Teach the person some alternative distractions to self-harm such as writing in a journal, listening to uplifting music, beating a pillow, screaming/shouting in a private place and/or exercising. Encourage using a red magic marker to draw on self (to represent the blood that would have flown), putting an ice cube in the crook of the elbow, defacing pictures in a catalog and/or letting Calgon take you away.

Remember, a self-injurer will stop self-abusive behavior only when the self-abus-

Self-Injurious Behaviors: Help Stop The Pain

er no longer finds it necessary to do so. In the meantime, nurturing and being "safe" is a caregiver's best bet for being part of the "cure".

I want to mention three books useful to my own emotional struggle with dealing with a cutter: (1) BODILY HARM: The Breakthrough Healing Process for Self-Injurers by Karen Conterio and Wendy Lader, Ph.D., (2) SECRET SCARS: Uncovering and Understanding the Addiction of Self-Injury by VJ Turner, and (3) SEE MY PAIN: Creative Strategies and Activities for Helping Young People Who Self-Injure by Susan Bowman, and Kaye Randall.

James still struggles with overwhelming emotions and remains vulnerable. Diane and I will do our best to be a support to him regardless of his choices. He knows that we love him and will do all we can to be there for him. He also knows that because we love him, we will at times hold him accountable for his choices, which he allows us to do because the trust is there.

Walk In A Manner Worthy

The following two poems are penned by James. They are a glimpse into his heart and soul.

Who Will Cry?

Who will cry for me?

For the boy beaten and bruised

Who will cry for me?

For the boy who's lost and confused

Who will cry for me?

For the boy who was touched where he didn't want to be

Who will cry for me?

For the boy sexually forced to touch another's body

Who will cry for me?

For the boy who was forced to wear his shit

Who will cry for me?

For the boy who had his face shoved in it

Who will cry for me?

For the boy forced to watch his dogs tortured and die

Who will cry for me?

For the boy who's truth was to live a lie

Who will cry for me?

For the boy who was afraid and bullied

Who will cry for me?

Who Will Cry

For the boy who ran away fearfully hurried

Who will cry for me?

For the boy who couldn't find a home

Who will cry for me?

For the boy in fear– feeling all alone

Who will cry for me?

For the boy who can't find his way

Who will cry for me?

For the boy who hurts each and every day

Who will cry for me?

For the boy no one seemed to like

Who will cry for me?

For the boy who had to fight

Who will cry for me?

For the boy who stole to have something nice

Who will cry for me?

For the boy using drugs to push away the pain

Who will cry for me?

For the boy who cuts himself to relieve his emotional strain

Who will cry for me?

For the boy living imprisoned inside his nightmares

Who will cry for me?

For the boy who dreams of death while everyone stares

Walk In A Manner Worthy

Who will cry for me?

For the boy who only relives his regret

Who will cry for me?

For the boy swallowing pride with anxiety's sweat

Who will cry for me?

For the boy who lost the only girl he truly loved

Who will cry for me?

For the boy who wants her back and begs the man above

Who will cry for me?

For the boy left behind with only a broken heart

Who will cry for me?

For the boy who failed when he tries so hard

Who will cry for me?

For the boy so depressed, reluctantly enduring another day

Who will cry for me?

For the boy who dreams of wings so he can fly far, far away

Who will cry for me?

For the boy who survives on anger and rage

Who will cry for me?

For the boy who trapped himself in the prison's cage

Who will cry for me?

For the boy desperately searching for love

Who will cry for me?

Who Will Cry

For the boy pushed away and shoved

Who will cry for me?

For the boy who was touched with hate

Who will cry for me?

For the boy who believes he's God's mistake

Who will cry for me?

For the boy who wants true love reality

Who will cry for me?

For the boy – will you cry for me?

Walk In A Manner Worthy

Only In My Dreams

To have all debts paid, money to burn,

Luxury to lie in, possessions allearned.

True love to share, by all means,

Quite possible, but only in my dreams.

A childhood worthwhile, fun, and untorn,

To not be terrified from the day I was born.

A father that was caring, loving and didn't scream,

All possible, but only in my dreams.

A mother not passive, angry, suicidal, and lost,

No scars, no bruises, no fears at any cost.

Nightmares gone, memories no more, sins all redeemed,

Quite possible, but only in my dreams.

A new family, emotions all refreshed,

No regrets, no fines – my wishes all caressed.

Good credit, no probation, my slate freshly cleaned,

Quite possible, but only in my dreams.

To grow up at home instead of being locked away,

Waking up on the right side of the bed every day.

To win the lottery, have no worries, a pocket full of green,

Quite possible, but only in my dreams.

To leave the country, no goodbyes, never come back.

Someone to listen, fully understand, and cut me some slack.

Only In My Dreams

To trust someone more than myself, a shoulder on which I can lean,

Quite possible, but only in my dreams.

No more struggles, complications, hatred and chaos,

Not be told, made to do anything, no one my boss.

All wishful thinking for so it should seem.

All quite possible, but still, only in my dreams.

Walk In A Manner Worthy

James' Testimony

This next read is from a collection of testimonials that Cornerstone Church of Ames, Iowa publishes every few years. A chain of events brought James to a breaking point that resulted in his surrendering his life to Christ. He starting attending Cornerstone, met some good role models and was later able to share his story. Julianne Faas, decided one individual was worthy of the church publication, and wrote the following article. This will give you more of a glimpse into the life of my son, not legally adopted by us, but a son in our hearts nonetheless.

"I should have died," said James Nieman. "Instead, God let me live after I overdosed causing my heart and liver to almost fail permanently." James went from intensive care, literally dying, to being healed within a week. After days of staring at the hospital walls, watching the I-V dripping, pulsing fluid in his veins, James wanted nothing more than to feel high.

His foster family had prayed for days asking God to spare his life, and He did. Meanwhile James ignored God. He had one goal, one mission, to please himself and get high. James harbored pain from his abusive childhood, guilt from his unruly behavior growing up and shame from ignoring, blaming and even hating God. He let his addiction once again take over his need to be numb and thus shot up first thing after leaving the hospital.

James fell flat on his face. As he felt the grass between his fingers he clawed at the ground. He was angry, bitter, tired; he finally had enough! He found himself on his hands and knees praying to Jesus, only because Kim Combes, his foster father, had told him so much about Him.

"Jesus I can't do this anymore! I hate my life! I hate my "friends"! I hate myself!" Then James felt something he had never felt before. He felt some peace and relief. "Thank you Jesus! I love you Jesus! Thank you Jesus! I need you Jesus! Jesus oh Jesus oh Jesus!" he said over and over while pacing back and forth in his front yard.

The Holy Spirit was so strong the guy using drugs with James also came to believe in Christ that night. Together they were thanking and praising God, high on drugs and out of their minds.

After his near death experience and an overwhelming love in his heart for once in his life, James cleaned up his life and began pursuing Christ. James was driven. He

James' Testimony

was connected with other Christians and read the Bible daily. He attended Cornerstone Church services, and for the first time in his life was non-violent in nature. He began to feel comfortable loving and trusting people. This lasted for about a year until James fell when he started a new relationship. As his love for her grew, he quickly faded out of Bible studies and church services. His new girlfriend met all his needs. She didn't judge him, or try to change him. She was not a Christian so she allowed him to drink heavily and do drugs while complementing his sexual nature.

His family and Christian friends reached out to James; they weren't okay with his destructive relationship. James felt God had sent them so they were able to convince him to end things. One night he asked her to leave. She took the dog, and went to stay with people with whom James didn't get along. Being a man who loved few things in his life that dog was a symbol of loyalty and love. When James arrived to take back his dog, confrontation arose and James lost it. He was instantly filled with so much rage he couldn't control himself. He literally beat the guy within an inch of his life. When he snapped out of it, he ran, only long enough to realize he had nowhere to go. When James turned himself in to the police, he later received a 25-year sentence.

James was remorseful; he knew he let God and his family down. In prison he read the entire Bible, underlining every passage that struck him. But it wasn't like before; he read, prayed, and studied the word but he never felt connected to God. He felt empty.

On Thanksgiving Day James was told he had a visitor. He was anxious as he walked across the prison yard, a place which he then considered home, and kept wondering who would be there to see him. Just before he entered the visitation room he saw his ex-girlfriend and his daughter through the glass in the door. His heart raced with excitement and rage as he met his daughter for the first time, yet he sat emotionless and silent. She was so small but so big. She was already two years old. James tried to hold his little girl for the first time but she was too scared of the stranger before her. She started to cry and reached for her mother. James continued to sit emotionless and silent. He didn't know how to respond. Reacting to his stoic nature, the mother cussed him up and down telling him he would never see his daughter again.

His blood was boiling! "I hated her and wished her dead." James walked back across the yard to his unit and sat alone. He started to tear up and his closest friends in prison with him noticed something was wrong. They tried to comfort him but he was beyond reach. After lashing out he took his Bible and threw it in the trash. He gave away his salvation. Within a couple days he picked a fight with an inmate to release his anger, and was subsequently transferred to another prison.

This transfer started the transformation God had planned for James. The new prison was filled with Christian inmates as well as some old friends James had met at the previous prison. His friends were different; they were full of love for God. "My brothers no longer had a hardness and hatred in their eyes. They were less confrontational and had compassion which was not there before. They seemed more at peace and had some happiness." He joined their Bible studies and started to feel God's grace again. "I didn't feel as angry or vengeful. I started to see where I was wrong and had to forgive or let go. I became more accepting of my powerlessness."

James got a new Bible and began to reread and remark every passage that spoke to him, all over again. In prison James completed his G.E.D. and earned certificates for eight programs, including a 32 week Bible Study course. He began apologizing to people he wronged, writing letters and asking people for forgiveness. God changed his heart.

James was called in for a VORP (Victim Offender Reconciliation Program) session at the request of the man he beat half to death. James listened to the man's testimony about how badly he was hurt. "This was very uncomfortable. But I felt compassion and regret for pain I caused this man." He was shocked when the man admitted he had taunted James. The VORP session was called because the man didn't feel the sentence James received was fair, His sentence went from 25 years down to 10. God was giving James a second chance. He became more productive and calm. At his first parole hearing, after serving three and a half years of the ten-year sentence, the parole board agreed it was time to release him.

Looking back James now sees how much he was pursued by God. He sees God as his aid, not his enemy. He works hard. Without the drugs he's clear minded and uses God's word to keep him on track. Last year his father apologized for the abuse in the past. James apologized, too, for acting out and belittling him as a father. He's restored the relationship with his biological family and still continues to be a solid member of the Combes family. James has built a strong unbreakable bond with his daughter, Lejla. He knows they can grow closer together in their love for Christ while attending Cornerstone.

James' Testimony

"I don't react with violence anymore, I resist temptation and even humble myself by loving and serving people whom I don't think deserve it," said James. "But I don't stand a chance without Him." It's a step-by-step process but Jesus is, indeed, healing the rage that once caged this man from within.

Letter From Adam

A few years back, while reading my email, the following was included in my daily influx of cyberspace messaging. Adam, one of James' best friends while he was living in my home, was someone I had heard of, but had never met even though, like Travis Lloyd, he'd been to my house. Rumor had it that Adam was a very intelligent young man who, like James (also intelligent), struggled with issues related to his own dysfunctional childhood.

It wasn't until after James turned 18, gave his life to Christ and was forging his own adult path, that I met Adam. Adam, too, had chosen recently to pursue the Christian walk. My family took to Adam immediately. My children loved and respected him, calling him "brother." Adam was and continues to be quite the charismatic young man. I frequently joked that he had such an ability to influence others that I was sure he could sell refrigerators to Eskimos.

In some ways, our deep late night talks, which were many over the time we've known him, intimidated me. I believed that Adam could think circles around me and thus challenged me in ways that only he could. Diane and I learned to love him more and more as we shared lives and vulnerabilities among us. In spite of not feeling like I could compete with him intellectually, I have a soft spot for him in my heart.

Adam lives on the edge. He is unpredictable at times. Not dangerous, but going for the gusto, striving for perfection. I have great admiration for Adam and while we don't communicate much anymore, I still see him on Facebook. Sometimes I have actually felt almost jealous that regardless of what he undertakes, he always seems to land on his feet. A great quality.

That said, the following is an example of what some of our conversations are like. Blunt, to the point, challenging. I asked his permission to use it because I believe we all need an Adam in our life. He is more than two decades my junior, but nonetheless, when we as elders allow the "Timothy's" of our lives to challenge us, we can come out on the other side of those exhortations better for it.

Thank you, Adam Henderson, for the influence you've been in my life. You know

Letter From Adam

I always wish for you the best. Loveya, Man!

Subject: Let's you and me face the hard truth:

We have to change and firmly stand for what we believe in. I am scared every day of being found out for a genuine lover and carer of people! I am scared everyday of being found out as a phony and misrepresentative of anything I stand for (due mostly to my pains and questions and thoughts, but.. If we claim this thing, this God, His Son, His freedom, His Glory, etc. than we cannot concede to the enemy in any of these cases we spoke of this morning! We cannot revel in one another's shames and guilts. We cannot every time be ensconced in brutal honesty only about our pitiful fleshy lives. We already know it sucks being human-we know it sucks being real and limited as well as selfish and unfulfilled. You are at a place I haven't arrived but I am not terribly far behind you on the larger scale! I know you hurt, I know you want justice and absolution (which in this case is Christ coming back) but, until then and only if you want this... You have to dig deeper and overcome those failings. You have all the tools and brains you need, you have the spirit and gifts available, just dig in and go after it. Show us, your kids, your brothers, your friends, your trusted ones, the world that depends on you without them even knowing they do-show them what it means to be a man of integrity and discipline, to be a man of stature and strength, to be a warrior who is unafraid of the battle and is ready unto death where you shall receive the full prize!

I need you. You can't fail me now. I don't claim you as one of my fathers in the faith for nothing. You have gone before me in so many ways and now is no time to hesitate. You are on the front lines every day and if not for you I myself might pull back or forget what living is about. Without your hand of love and grace and mercy who are the rest of us to be? You have helped calm the hearts of men throughout your life and would you halt now? Look at James.. He would not be who he is without you! Look at the countless others! Dad...James, Matt and guys like us will always have problems (we all have em) but now is not the time to attach yourself to those problems. You must love the sinner and hate the sin. Always the same concept, just sometimes it gets real personal. You did what you could and now you let us go. Life moves on. God is still God, He is still the unchanging perfection that we all desire but

Walk In A Manner Worthy

it does get harder and that is when we draw nearer! We come to the cross-we arrive and we hold fast. Pick up your stick, your wood, your tree and carry it man. Help me carry mine and allow me to offer the same services when I can. We are in it together in Him-without Him we are all for one and none for all.

You mean the world to me and have shaped me and if we are both unsatisfied then we move forward and claim the better deal. We move forward and achieve what was never possible with the old us, the old paradigms, the old actions. We move forward in Grace because with all this charging we will fall and grow tired. We might faint-it is ok. We get up and roll out once again.

Love your wife if you really love her, love your kids if you really love them and selflessness will be your reward. A greater love that you understand when no one else does is your reward. Sacrifice is the greatest reward for all great men who seek purity, love and righteousness. Do you think the men who come home from battle and get their Silver Stars, their Medals of Honor, their Purple Hearts care about that "piece" of material? No, they are only thinking of how they loved their companion, their friend, their partner, those who depended on them and even sometimes their enemy. We all have jobs to do and that is what is called of the flesh every day. We die to this nature and gain a brilliant gleaming satisfying hope that transcends thought, heart and the understanding of both.

We can only create so many ideas and so many paths for our feet to walk and stay comfortable but in the end it all gives way to whatever foundation was formed, to whatever we have built as framework that cannot be torn away.. We can always re-pour and repave. We can always grab new lumber and rebuild what has been broken.

I have watched my real father and mother lose the battle too often to not stand up and tell you how much I love and need you. Stay in the game, Dad, and let's play some ball! You are more of a man than you know and you need to bank on discovering the rest of what's in you. You have much left and there is no time like the present to dig it out.
Have a beautiful weekend and take your time... but don't be afraid - never be afraid.
I love you,
-A

No Regrets

Over the course of years, I have been tremendously blessed with great relationships and opportunities to share my faith with others. This story has never been published until now although I wrote it over two decades ago. It is reflective of yet another way God showed Himself to me through an interaction I had with a local young man shortly after moving to a small town with the four young men in my charge. "Mike" was one of several young people from town that frequently chilled out at my home in his spare time.

This scenario fluctuates back and forth in "flashback" fashion from one scene to another. It is my desire that this will not be a distraction, but rather a creative way to juggle the story in a more dramatic way. As mentioned, it's never been published, but nonetheless, for me it still rings of the lesson I learned from Mike being in my life. Let me now introduce you to Mike:

The call came at 11:00 P.M. "Kim, met me in front of the auction house in two minutes. I'll see you there." I knew from the distinct sound that he was on his cell phone.

My house was quiet - finally. The four foster teens with whom I share my home were settling down in each of their own rooms while I was awaiting their visit from the Sandman. I could slip out for a few minutes to discover why Mike wanted me to venture only two blocks from my home when he usually drops in when a talk was needed. The urgency in his voice roused my curiosity.

Mike, a good-humored, seemingly caring young man was first introduced to me a couple months prior to his senior year of high school. Having gregarious adolescent boys in my foster home set the stage for me interacting with a good percentage of the teens around town. Mike's demeanor was pleasant and easy-going - a breath of fresh air when the ones that lived here were anything but. We did not spend much time talking, but he was always polite and asked how things were going for me.

An autumn conflict with one of my charges deterred him from returning to the house for spontaneous casual conversation with those of us who lived here. Since the cessation of his social calls, I heard his name off and on around the house. He was thus "gone, but not forgotten." It was at the start of the next summer that I had opportunity to meet Mike's younger brother. When I realized who Tom was, I asked him to deliver a message to his older sibling. "Tell him he can come back again now that his antagonist no longer lives here."

On the evening of July 5, Mike reappeared. He didn't exactly know why he stopped, just that Tom had given him my message; he was driving by - so what the heck! It was 11:00 PM. Neither of us realized that the discussion that would eventuate would be life-changing for Mike. Five and a half hours later Mike left my home with a new view of life. In my challenging his worldview and his thinking about God, Jesus, and other religious beliefs, this recently turned 18 year-old man gave his life to Christ. In subsequent weeks, this new believer visited often for encouragement and prayer. He was now challenging my guys to re-evaluate their belief system as it related to their eternal destiny and current lifestyles. One could glean from his conversations that Mike was a "new creation."

My annual week-long vacation at my friend's cabin on Lake Okoboji was approaching in October. In relating this to Mike one night as we shared our faith, he (who hadn't had a vacation in quite some time and was wanting to get out of town for a while) asked if he could travel with me to enjoy the serenity of which I spoke - past experiences at Linda's summer home affectionately and appropriately called "Grace Place." It was decided I would have a cabin mate this year as I celebrated my favorite season - Fall - at the Iowa Great Lakes in the northwest part of the state.

The headlights of my Caravan cast on the wall behind them the distinct silhouette of a couple sitting on the curb in front of the auction house. I don't know what I was expecting when I arrived, but I knew this wasn't it. Voices carrying emotional upset through the chilly September night air gave evidence of an argument not yet near resolution. My presence was acknowledged by two swift glances upward, but the heated discussion missed not a beat. Trying to analyze the situation, I was still uncertain as to the role I was to play in this already-in-progress scenario.

A pause in the conversation gave Mike the opportunity to bring me up to speed as to why my presence was summoned shortly after 11:00 on this Tuesday night. Apparently a stalemate had been reached between Mike and Michelle, his ex-girlfriend of about one week. They had dated for almost two years and Mike had believed, for right now anyway, that a redefining of the relationship was needed. He believed,

No Regrets

albeit over-optimistically, that I could help them through the impasse so as to transition more smoothly into a "just friends" relationship.

As I listened to the words and intensity on both sides, it became clear to me that my past was slapping me in the face. The conflict between Mike and Michelle was reminiscent of those occurring between me and my former girlfriends of years gone by. It was a painful realization when I heard Michelle accusing Mike of his real and/or perceived faults in communication techniques and style. Because of this, and because I was asked to by Mike, I spoke the truth - truth that Mike did not want to hear.

One could visibly see the emotional walls go up as I expounded upon my perception of their current situation. Mike made it abundantly clear that he was done talking. While telling him if he changed his mind he knew where I lived, I picked myself up from a sitting position on the curb to leave. Unexpectedly, as I walked past him to enter my vehicle, he surprisingly pulled me into a close embrace as he said "thank you." It was almost two weeks until I realized what that was about.

Twelve nights passed. Mike came to the house to do our usual catch-up and encouraging of one another. In the course of conversation, I asked him about that night - why the hug? It was as he told me the story of his mother and grandfather that the profundity of his thinking and subsequent "hug decision" ingrained in me the necessity of his action.

It had been his mother's exhortation to him to never part company on a bad note with someone for whom you care. Years earlier, she and her father had gotten into an argument. Pride kept her from reconciling in a timely manner. Death suddenly snatched her dad without even so much as a warning to right the wrongs and exchange "I love you's" - a memory she never forgot. In an attempt to pass this lesson to posterity, she had taught her now-18-year-old son to mend fences as quickly as possible so he would not experience the heartache of a never-healed broken relationship. The gravity of Mom's irrefutable lesson had surely made an impact on her offspring's young sensitive heart.

The cabin was, as always, an oasis in an otherwise hectic workaday world. It was great to "veg out" with no schedule to follow, few chores needing to be done, no persons demanding attention from either of us. While nippy outside, the inside temperature was still fairly cozy, even without structural insulation or a furnace to take the chill off. The laid-back atmosphere invited joking around, laughter and casual conversation. However, one topic eventually lead to heightened emotions as my challenging of his ideas and beliefs hit closer to home than was comfortable for Mike. Once more, I was able to watch the walls go up and was told he was done talking for right now. He left the deck overlooking the lake and entered into warmer temperatures.

It was as I surveyed the choppy whitecaps before me that I decided I wanted (or needed) a walk. Meanwhile, Mike's example to me near the auction house a month prior popped into my brain. It seemed God was convicting me of my need to break the ice so that Mike would know that regardless of his attitude towards me, my love for him was still unconditional.

He was less than 15 feet away, separated from me by a heavy glass deck door. I rose from the white wicker chair on which I was sitting and breathed deeply as I slid open the glass door between us. Mike was slouched, dejected-looking, in an easy chair ahead of me. Apprehensive of how he might respond, I risked the "no regrets" method I learned from him less than 30 days ago. I informed him I would be taking an evening stroll. Before I left, however, I wanted to share with him something that I learned recently from someone important to me. "In case I get hit by a car and don't come back, I just want you to know that 'I love ya, Man!'"

A quick grin flashed across his face. A short conversation followed as I left for my 3 mile prayer walk. I spent this time asking God to show Mike how to walk with Him. Also, I asked for wisdom for me as to how to best challenge Mike's (or anyone's) thinking with "heavy-duty, eternal-destiny, walking-with-Jesus" type questions.

Moreover, I asked God to keep me ever mindful to utilize this "no regrets" communication tool learned by me from a sagacious 18 year-old who learned it as a youngster on his mother's knee. Life is indeed too short not to make peace between family and friends. No one knows when that last angry word or gesture during a conflict with a loved one will be the very last.

As A Foster Parent

I cannot recall where I found this, but the words reassured me that no matter the strength of my desire to better the life of any teen in my home, I could do only so much. I had to let go...

As A Foster Parent...

I can give you a family in which to live, but I cannot make it your home.

I can teach you things, but I cannot make you learn.

I can give you directions, but I cannot be there to lead you.

I can allow you freedom, but I cannot account for it.

I can take you to church, but I cannot make you believe.

I can teach you right from wrong, but I cannot always decide for you.

I can buy you beautiful clothes, but I cannot make you beautiful inside.

I can offer you advice, but I cannot accept it for you.

I can give you love, but I cannot force it upon you.

I can teach you to share, but I cannot make you unselfish.

I can teach you respect, but I cannot force you to show honor.

I can advise you about friends, but cannot choose them for you.

I can advise you about sex, but I cannot keep you pure.

I can tell you the facts of life, but I cannot build your reputation.

I can tell you about drink, but I cannot say "no" for you.

I can warn you about drugs, but I cannot prevent you from using them.

I can tell you about lofty goals, but I cannot achieve them for you.

I can teach you about kindness, but I cannot force you to be gracious.

I can warn you about sins, but I cannot make you moral.

Walk In A Manner Worthy

I can love you as a child, but I cannot make you want me as a parent.

I can pray for you, but I cannot make you make good choices.

I can tell you how to live, but I cannot give you a good adult life now or in the future

I can come along beside you, but I can't take away your pain.

Author unknown

God's Kisses On the Forehead

God's "kisses on the forehead" - that's what I call out-of-the-blue, random things happening that encourage my heart. These "kisses" can come at any time, and oh when they do, they are sooo sweet.

Diane and I were at the Houston airport several years ago waiting to catch a plane back to Iowa. We had been gone several days and were anxious to get back home after a couple days of presenting at a foster care conference. After a prolonged wait there was a sudden change in departure time and gate. All those headed to Des Moines were told to grab belongings to now go wait at yet another point at Bush International.

Among those heading to Iowa was a 40-something Asian woman, who, by the look of her body language, was greatly confused. She had no idea what was happening. I approached her, held out my boarding pass then pointed to hers so I could ascertain her next destination. She indeed was heading to Iowa. I gestured and said "come with me" waving my arm and hand in a forward motion. She smiled, bowed towards me to say "thank you" and we eventually made it to Des Moines.

Fast forward two months. I was having a great pity-party as I picked up some groceries from our local Aldi store. My heart was heavy contemplating whether I was making any difference in the lives of our children and some clients who were struggling. Positive change was slow in coming and I really felt despairing - ready to throw in the towel and quit expending any more energy reaching out, thus acquiescing to the helpless and powerless emotions I was experiencing. "God, I need a refreshment of soul. Toss me a bone, something I can hang my hat on to show me that my labor for You is not in vain."

As I picked up some various fruits I noticed three women of Asian descent seemingly staring at me. One was whispering to an older lady - perhaps her mother - then looking back at me. As I got closer to them, the younger of the two said "I know you" and kept pointing at me. I smiled, shrugged and responded that I thought she was mistaken. She became more adamant and animated, getting a tad louder even, repeating "I know you". Then she said "Houston" and repeated. Still clueless I shook my head no. In broken English she said "You say 'Come with me. Come with me!'" While waving to me as I had done with her two months previously. The power of this kiss was so great that right in the middle of Aldi tears welled up and ran down my cheek. God whispered "You made a difference, my son." (Interestingly, even as I write these words tears are welling again as I vividly recall how that "kiss on the forehead" lifted the fog and hopelessness I had been feeling just seconds before she spoke).

My most recent God kiss came yesterday, but before I share this story, I have to relate some background information. Fifteen years ago I was employed as an in-home therapist for a local private agency. I had the privilege of serving many clients caught up in the throes of struggles that landed them in "the system." Javier was no exception.

Admittedly I was a tad apprehensive about meeting this young man in his early 20's. Along with his paperwork, I received word he was not thrilled with Caucasian counselors. I was stepping into a culture much different than my own, hoping any fear on my part would not be noticed by Javier. Our initial meeting took place on a picnic table in the center of town...just in case.

As a man of faith I always pray prior to a session, sometime during the meeting and always afterwards. For this particular get-together I was more fervent than usual in petitioning the Lord. While he came off somewhat cocky at first, my defenses were down very shortly after shaking hands. This man, of whom it was rumored didn't like white guys, especially those with some power and authority over him, presented as personable and friendly. We actually hit it off very well (thank you, God). His charm was one of his greatest strengths in forming a rapport with each other. After a couple hours sharing life experiences he agreed to meet with me again the following week.

As time passed he became more open, more vulnerable. Javier shared with me that his girlfriend, with whom he had children, was amazed he liked me. Laughing, he told me that he was amazed he liked me.

At one our sessions (our last, unbeknownst to me at the time), we met with his two children at a local fast food restaurant. The youngsters played in the area with the colored balls while we conversed. We were discussing his proclivity towards alcohol, especially beer. By this time he knew I was a Christian as contrary to the "rules of social work" I had shared parts of my life with him also - my testimony was one of them. When asked if I could, Javier agreed to let me pray with him. I thus asked God, out loud with him, to take away his desire and added "please make him sick any time he tries to drink it." He found this to be quite humorous as there was no way he would ever conceive of a time he would hate beer.

God's Kisses On the Forehead

A few days later I received word that he had gotten arrested and was probably going to prison for a crime he had yet to be tried as his court date had been pending. I do not remember all the details after 15 years, but I remember feeling sad as I saw huge potential in this young man after having worked with him over the last few months. I wondered what God was going to do in and through him to get his attention.

Several weeks passed when one day I got a letter from him at my office. Javier was incarcerated at a state prison. He gave me details as to how he was doing and humbly asked if there was any chance I could come meet with him again. Too, he informed me that my prayers were powerful. After our last session he had gone home and later opened a beer. He took one swallow and spit it out. He could no longer tolerate the taste – just as I had specifically asked God to do.

Time passed and I did indeed visit him in prison where I also got to meet his family whom I had not yet met. They were warm and inviting towards me. His parents had heard about me, this man of faith, and were delighted I took an interest in their wayward son. His siblings were cautious and observed me somewhat incredulously, seemingly wondering why a dorky white guy would come visit an Hispanic man in prison.

Javier and I kept in touch. When he had served his sentence he asked if he could come visit me at my home. Although at one time he had been a client, I said yes as now he was a friend. He considered me a mentor and I was delighted to serve him in that capacity. He brought with him his girlfriend and his adorable infant son who had been born a few months after his arrest. Javier made a hit with my family and we shared good conversation for a few hours in our home. They returned home and I then lost track of him.

Over a decade has passed. I had occasionally searched for Javier online but to no avail. His birthday is a day after a friend's so I always remembered it and yearly think about him, wondering how he's faring in the world.

He celebrated his birthday a few weeks ago. In thinking about him, I shared the beer prayer story with a friend. Two weeks later I received a form in the mail asking me permission for Javier to make contact with me. He was back in a state prison. I immediately completed this paperwork and sent it back, excited that he had once again reached out – that he was alive and wanting to again interact.

Walk In A Manner Worthy

Yesterday I received a letter detailing in Reader's Digest style the events of his life the last 1.5 decades. He had made some poor decisions ultimately landing him behind bars yet again, but some good things were happening as a result. (Coincidently, while writing this paragraph Javier called from prison and we were able to talk for about 10 minutes...the first time in over thirteen years). He informed me he had memorized my address years ago and had never forgotten it. He had even over the years driven by the house several times...honking, but was afraid to stop. He further reported that he would be returning to civilian life next month and already had some good job possibilities. He had hope for the future.

So, the "kiss on the forehead"? Several, actually. Just knowing Javier was alive and again reaching out for help and support was the first one. Receiving the phone call while I was in process of relating this story was greatly encouraging to me also. Lastly, the contents of his letter which reminded me yet again that God created me for His glory, to serve His purposes in loving others, reflecting to the best of my ability the attributes of Jesus to those that need love, support and ongoing encouragement as they fight their personal battles. Too, having a whole decade pass was yet another reminder to me that we can plant seeds daily, but the harvest comes when God says it comes. Just because we get impatient about how we think life should unfold, doesn't mean that fruit will not eventually come. Javier's letter, here in part, is proof of this.

> "Wow! It seems just yesterday we sat at that {restaurant} in the play area and you ruined my love for alcohol! Thank you! FYI, I haven't drank a beer since then. True story. Have never been able to get over the smell. I have so much I want to catch up on with you and I promise you, you're now stuck with me for the rest of my life. LOL.
>
> I've thought A LOT of you over the years and always wanted to reach out to you but to be very honest with you I was scared you'd pray for me and ruin all the "fun" I thought I was having. I wish I would've never lost contact with you. I believe I wouldn't be where I'm at now if I had kept you in my life.
>
> Mr. Combes, I'm writing to you because I not only need your prayers but I want you to be in my life and to help me become the man and the father

God's Kisses On the Forehead

I know I can be. I will put all the work in if you are willing to help me. Please, for me and my children!

   Love,

   Javier"

So there you have it, folks. Don't dismiss your purpose on this planet. You make a difference. Regardless of feelings of inadequacy or inferiority, God will use you.

"Therefore, brethren, stand firm. Let nothing move you. Always give yourself fully to the work of the Lord for you know your labor in the Lord is NOT IN VAIN"
(I Corinthians 15:58)

Walk In A Manner Worthy

The Black Dot

Imagine, if you will, a white board one would see in any high school or college classroom setting. You enter this room, grab a seat and quickly notice in the far right hand side of this board a black dot about 2 inches in diameter. The board is clear of any markings save this dot.

I have the honor of being certified to present the Nurtured Heart Approach (NHA), the brainchild of Howard Glasser, who personally led a week-long train-the-trainers seminar in Iowa seven years ago. While I was initially skeptical of this new paradigm, I soon came to the realization that this methodology was something I needed in my toolbox four decades previous. Mercy and grace exemplified. Both imperative in dealing with children lacking social skills and socially acceptable behaviors.

It is not within the scope of this article to go into great detail about the structure of NHA and how it works. That concept might become another article or book down the road, however. It is my purpose at this time to not only illustrate an idea that challenged my thinking seven years ago but simultaneously challenge others' thinking as well.

Of the many slides included in my NHA presentation one is of a white space showing a black dot in the upper corner. Upon projecting said slide for the audience, I ask "What is it you see here?" A humble question that many perceive as possibly more tricky than it is. Simply put, it's a white board with a black dot, which in and of itself means nothing in relationship to working with challenging children and teens. However, once I explain it from the NHA perspective, it creates yet another tool able to assist our charges to realize more fully the gifts inherent in their personalities. Let me expound.

As humans, we more easily lean towards seeing negative traits in ourselves and in others rather than the positive characteristics which we all possess in spite of the fact we may have to delve deeper in some than in others. The black dot represents all the things our kids do that irritate and frustrate us, that go against societal norms and mores, things that might even embarrass us as parents and caregivers when demonstrated in a public arena. These are the glaring behaviors which result in complaints in the home, in the school and in the community.

The white portion, furthering the analogy, reflects all the things our charges do "right" for which they get little emotional credit, if any at all. Yes, our hurting and

The Black Dot

angry youth may have a long repertoire of less-than-desirable behaviors that tend to overshadow any good choices made through the course of any given day; however, how guilty are we in not noticing the actions that reflect and demonstrate their inner wealth?

I once had a client, the father of two young lads, who adamantly refused to give any positive encouragements towards the boys when they completed their homework, took out the trash without complaining, brushed their teeth in a timely fashion each night and so on. His rationale was that these were things expected of them and he wasn't going out of his way to compliment them for doing what was right and expected as members of his family. He was, however, quick to anger when his sons did not meet up to his parental standards, thus he was reinforcing a very negative "I'm not enough" sullied self-image.

When I reminded him he was indeed an avid sports fan and as such, showed jubilant excitement when his teams of choice played well and won their games. This, of course, gave him pause. He comprehended that he became fanatical and quite animated in his affect when his heroes did "what they were expected to do" which of course was to give all for the team, sometimes at great sacrifice to themselves. The intended point was duly noted by my client.

How many sports teams would acquiesce to the opposing teams' talents if their fans refused to jump and cheer in the stands, but instead played cards amongst themselves as the team exerted energy to attempt a win? How many rock stars would finish a concert if no one hollered, danced, raised their cell phones or crooned to familiar tunes? I would venture that the most popular of all stars would, at minimum, contemplate walking off the stage if they could not get audience participation within 15 minutes. Too, I'd bet money every reader of this book yearns for recognition at work, in their immediate or extended families and as a community member.

All this to say: we most definitely need cheerleaders, someone who believes in us – sometimes against all odds. We need unconditional love based solely on our identity of who we are, not conditional love founded on what we may or may not accomplish. After all, we are human beings, not human doings.

Realistically most people perform far more positive behaviors opposed to overwhelmingly adverse behaviors damaging to self or others. What could happen if we trained ourselves to be on the lookout for behaviors we can encourage in our children and in others? Too much emotional energy for undesirable behaviors could backfire producing more undesirable behaviors. "How could that happen?" you might ask. Great question.

The subsequent reward for exuding negative emotion is juicy, albeit not helpful, relationship with the individual with whom there is conflict. We can counter this from happening by utilizing strong intentionality when we contribute less energy to the behaviors we don't want, and more towards the actions we do want. For example, if a child gets a fifteen minute lecture on the pros and cons of respecting vs. disrespecting persons of authority but only a three second "Hey, thanks for taking out the trash so quickly" (accompanied with a high-five), which behavior will the child more likely choose in the future to get the most relational bang for their buck?

Back to the white board. Your 4 year old foster son, easily triggered, has a meltdown about having to pick up his toys. Typically, he throws himself down or stomps around the living room. However, this particular time he sits himself in the middle of the floor and just cries. We know, even at four, he has many choices, good and bad, to choose from when he's upset. One of them, which he has done in the past, is to tip over the coffee table. He did not do this, nor did he even look at the table in contemplation of such an act. Thus, when he is done crying, you cheerfully give him eye contact and state something like this: "Wow, you were really angry, but you did not even go close to the table, you didn't throw yourself on the floor nor did you stomp around the room, when the truth is, you could have. This shows me that you are learning self-control and showing respect to a great degree." Awkward? Uncomfortable? Realistic, even? Yes to all.

I fully realize this is not old school parenting. Remember, however, it is against the law to use corporal punishment on a child in foster care. But even if it wasn't, it would not be a good plan. These children are already traumatized and used to physical and/or sexual abuse. They trust no one. Another spanking for bad behavior only reinforces to them, yet again, their caregivers are out to hurt them.

Utilizing the NHA methodology de-escalates the situation in both child and parent, while instilling in the child the encouragement that he or she has what it takes to follow the rules, as evidenced by NOT doing the destructive options mentioned above. Yes, it takes some getting used to, but when practiced with consistency, this methodology has been proven to be effective in changing dysfunctional dynamics of both children and caregivers in diverse settings i.e. homes, schools, day care centers, residential facilities, etc.

The Black Dot

Shortly after learning this NHA technique, I started practicing with fervency, seeing positive results in my home and with clients. An almost magical transformation started happening when I remembered to use this new paradigm rather than revert back to less effective methods. I'll give a personal example for more clarification.

My 17-year-old son, Jordan (whom we'd adopted with his three siblings when he was 6 years of age) and I went out to a local lake to talk one night early into his senior year of high school. Historically, we both had our share of frustrations and conflicts with the other and I felt thus prompted to take a risk in being vulnerable - just the two of us to discuss issues I believed needed addressed as he stepped on the threshold of adulthood. In the course of our 3-plus hour conversation that evening, I had him envision the white board with the black dot. I did not anticipate what was to follow.

I apologized and asked forgiveness for the times, in frustration, I refused, consciously or unconsciously, to see all his great qualities, which were many in actuality. This young man was super athletically inclined. He had a great sense of humor. He was able to interact positively with almost anyone, if he chose to do so. He had a great ability to persevere in the face of many obstacles to his goals in life. I asked him to forgive me for focusing on the black dot, and not on all the things he did well, or those actions he could have done, but didn't, such as getting in trouble with the law, skipping classes, do drugs, etc. Jordan verbalized that he did, indeed, forgive me. I thanked him and we hugged.

It started getting late and chilly - thus time to head back home for bed. Before we left, however, Jordan said, "Dad, I need to ask you something. Will YOU forgive ME for all the times that I made choices that hurt you and Mom?"

Time stopped. I was speechless. Tears welled in my eyes (although being dark, I doubt he saw them). This conversation was going down in the history books for me. He had been my son for over a decade and this was THE first time I could remember that he had ever apologized for anything - and, in my head anyway, he had plenty to apologize for. This was not, however, a time to remind him of this. This situation called for humility, something that was difficult for both of us. I am totally convinced that his request for forgiveness would not have come had I not modeled it first, exposing my parental vulnerable side, which is something I believe all young people need from us as parents. How will they know it's okay to do this if we, their role-models, don't demonstrate how it's done?

The Black Dot

I don't usually give homework assignments at the end of my missives, but I'm going to make an exception here. In closing, I challenge every reader to bring to mind one or more individuals whom you could take out for pizza, to an arcade, or to a lake with the sole purpose of doing exactly what I did with Jordan. I know that every reader has something for which an expression of regret is due. How do I know this? Because you're all human! You're fallible. You've blown it with your kids. Your pride got in the way of healthy juicy relationship.

I remember many years ago I presented an anger de-escalation workshop where I invited the audience to think of a time when they, as parents, knew an apology needed to be offered on their part. I challenged them to take the risk of asking forgiveness, regardless of how long it had been since the offense took place. One man, probably in his early 60's, told me he would not take that challenge as he was sure his children would lose all respect for him if he showed weakness...vulnerability. Honestly, I was taken aback by his response. I could not convince him, though, that I believed they would have MORE respect for him for this act, not less.

This exercise I propose will invite healing. Don't let pride dictate non-action here. It's up to you. The time is now. I'm willing to wager it will open up doors to communication like no other, or at least plant a seed for something good down the road. Take me up on it. And know I'd love to hear how it went.

Here's to the healing. CHEERS!

Little Annie

I first read this story back in the early 90's. So powerful was its impact that I never forgot it. I have used it occasionally to conclude my training sessions, sometime seeing tears in the eyes of the audience upon completion of the reading.

Take it to heart, readers, take it to heart. You make a difference.

At the turn of the twentieth century there was an asylum in the suburbs of Boston which dealt with severely mentally retarded and disturbed individuals. One of the patients was a girl who was simply called Little Annie. She was totally unresponsive to others in the asylum. The staff tried everything they could to help her, yet without success. Finally she was confined to a cell in the basement of the asylum and given up as hopeless.

But a beautiful Christian woman worked at the asylum, and she believed that every one of God's creatures needed love, concern and care. So she decided to spend her lunch hours in front of Little Annie's cell, reading to her and praying that God would free her from her prison of silence. Day after day the Christian woman came to Little Annie's door and read, but the little girl made no response. Months went by. The woman tried to talk with Little Annie, but it was like talking to an empty cell. She brought little tokens of food for the girl, but they were never received.

Then one day a brownie was missing from the plate which the caring woman retrieved from Little Annie's cell. Encouraged, she continued to read to her and pray for her. Eventually the little girl began to answer the woman through the bars of her cell. Soon the woman convinced the doctors that Little Annie needed a second chance at treatment. They brought her up from the basement and continued to work with her. Within two years Little Annie was told that she could leave the asylum and enjoy a normal life.

But she chose not to leave. She was so grateful for the love and attention she was given by the dedicated Christian woman that she decided to stay and love others as she had been loved. So Little Annie stayed on at the institution to work with other patients who were suffering as she had suffered.

Walk In A Manner Worthy

Nearly half a century later, the Queen of England held a special ceremony to honor one of America's most inspiring women, Helen Keller. When asked to what she would attribute her success at overcoming the dual handicap of blindness and deafness, Helen Keller replied, "If it hadn't been for Ann Sullivan, I wouldn't be here today."

Ann Sullivan, who tenaciously loved and believed in an incorrigible blind and deaf girl named Helen Keller, was Little Annie. Because one selfless Christian woman in the dungeon of an insane asylum believed that a hopeless little girl needed God's love, the world received the marvelous gift of Helen Keller.

Excerpt from VICTORY OVER DARKNESS (Chap. 5 p. 87) by Neil T. Anderson

My Worst "Best" Christmas Ever

I wrote the following over a quarter century ago. It has since been published in numerous news outlets including The Des Moines Register (Iowa's largest circulated newspaper) on December 25, 2008. I update this annually to keep it timely as well as post it every Christmas Eve on my Facebook wall. It is my hope that it has touched lives in ways that I might never know on this side of eternity. My faith, my walk is foundational to everything I do. Without God, I am nothing. May He be glorified in the writing of, and reading of, this piece and in the entire book as a whole.

Thank you, Jesus, for pulling me out of darkness so I can be a light to those whom you want me to serve.

"WHY??? What is the meaning of it all?" I demanded of God in desperation as I contemplated my earthly purpose on this Christmas Eve 1975. Only the glow of the fluorescent bulbs in the hollowed-out cross gave light to my life as I sat alone in the sanctuary of the church I had attended since Jr. High. My spirit was broken as I observed and felt the pain of living. As a senior in high school, I was caught in a world of deteriorating relationships, drugs, alcohol, pornography and a self-loathing that I could not escape. I wanted out...out of life itself. Hot tears of anger streamed down my cheeks as I poured my heart to a God that seemed distant and unreal to me. "Where are you?" I begged of this entity, as my hopeless world seemed to collapse around me. My emotional turmoil was exacerbated by the fact it was Christmas and holiday goodwill and cheer were as distant from my soul as I believed God was.

Christmas Day brought no relief. Gifts of love meant nothing. My family watched and wondered why I was so reticent, my vacuous appearance frightening them. Grandma, overwhelmingly empathetic and afraid, cried observing the obvious depression that clung to me like a wet blanket.

Suicide. That was the answer. The family car...drive 90 miles per hour into a bridge...that should do it. Tears wouldn't stop as I got behind the wheel, thinking I would never again see anyone I loved. But what if I didn't die? What if I was comatose or a quadriplegic for the next 60 years? What if the Bible was right? Heaven? Hell? Baby Jesus? The Cross? Shed blood for my sins? Questions...many, but no answers.

Walk In A Manner Worthy

"GOD!!!" I screamed as I continued to drive aimlessly. "I don't even know if You exist, but if You are there and Jesus is who the Bible says he is, PLEASE...forgive me. Come into my life. Make me who YOU want me to be. I am a failure. Make me new." My fist was raised as I dared yell at the heavens, my heart as broken as I had ever known. Nothing. No voices. No visions. No angels. No answers. Just tears and the weight of heart-crushing sadness. No suicide. Fear of the unknown kept me alive.

Two days pass. The mail arrives. Not one, but two copies of Billy Graham's book PEACE WITH GOD. From where? From whom? Why now? The timing seemed impeccable. As I read, I truly enjoyed a peace I'd never felt before. The Bible, too, was coming alive as I hungrily studied for truth. Could this be it? Could Jesus, this Baby of Old, be the answer? Could it be this simple? Skepticism kept me cautious. Time would tell.

Forty-five years have passed since my miracle of Christmas. The 'worst' Yuletide I had ever experienced became in retrospect, the 'greatest' Christmas in my 60's as the author delved into Fish's psyche and his subsequent bizarre behaviors years. The Babe in the Manger gave me the peace and joy that eluded me my teen years. Yes, I still struggle when trials come my way. I am light years from being perfect. But for the last 45 years, this Christmas Baby has been my Friend, my Rock, my Anchor, my Redeemer, and the Lover of my Soul.

The innkeeper in the Book of Luke didn't have room. Will our society, too, continue to say, "no room at the inn"? This Christmastime let us let Jesus be born in the stable of our hearts. Let His love inundate the emptiness and brokenness of our souls, our families, our workplaces and our country. This is my fervent prayer this Christmas season and into the coming year.

I am proof positive that a wreck of a life can indeed be transformed and healing can take place. God, in the form of Emmanuel, was the Answer to my questions.

Happy Birthday, Baby Jesus!!!

My Worst "Best" Christmas Ever

Dear Reader, If you have read up to this point and have felt led to confess sin and dedicate yourself to the One Living God, may I invite you to consider these four passages from the Book of Romans, the Passion Translation.

(3:23) For we all have sinned and are in need of the glory of God.

(6:23) For sin's meager wages is death, but God's lavish gift is life eternal, found in your union with our Lord Jesus, the Anointed One.

(10:9-10) And what is God's "living message"? It is the revelation of faith for salvation, which is the message that we preach. For if you publicly declare with your mouth that Jesus is Lord and believe in your heart that God raised him from the dead, you will experience salvation. The heart that believes in him receives the gift of the righteousness of God—and then the mouth gives thanks to salvation.

(10:13) And it's true: "Everyone who calls on the name of the Lord Yahweh will be rescued and experience new life."

Are you willing to step out in faith to receive forgiveness for all your sins, have a secure place with Jesus in heaven, freedom from guilt and shame coupled with strength to live victoriously in our chaotic world? This simple prayer prayed with a sincerely repentant heart will assure you of those very things.

Jesus, I believe that You made me and want me to follow You with all my heart. I know I have disobeyed and have wanted to be my own boss. I have thought and done things against Your directions, thus I know I am a sinner and I ask for Your forgiveness. I believe You died on the cross for my sins and rose from the dead. I turn from my sins and invite You to come into my heart and life. I want to trust and obey You as my Lord and Savior. I need You. I open the door of my life and receive You as my Savior and Lord. Thank You for forgiveness and giving me eternal life. Please take control of the throne of my life. I accept your promises and ask you to please keep me in Your love and care now and forever. Please transform me into the person You want me to be. I pray all this in Your holy Name. Amen.

Welcome to the Family. We'll meet someday on the other side of eternity. My prayers are with you. In Jesus' Name.

Walk In A Manner Worthy

Speaking Endorsements

Anyone who has ever attended one of my presentations has heard me state that I absolutely DO NOT do trainings that I cannot passionately proclaim, that I don't believe in. I will never present material I read in a book or learned in a class just so I can acquire a paycheck. I will not waste an audience's time, nor my own, to ramble on for 6 hours to be X amount of dollars richer afterwards. If I'm at the podium, know the information is important to me and I want it to be important to the attendees also. That said, I posted on Facebook (and in some cases asked directly) that I was looking for anyone from any of my several classes who would be willing to compose an evaluation paragraph or two for me. Many more than I expected charitably responded to my request.

The following quips are both unashamedly and unabashedly posted here for advertising purposes. Procuring speaking gigs is the vehicle for putting bread and butter on my family table while simultaneously allowing me to pass on what I believe is cutting-edge information needed to do the work of healing the heart of a challenging child in any setting.

Too, I want readers to know up front that I did not pay anyone to write what each has written. I couldn't have shelled out enough money to get the kudos I so generously received here. Because my love language is "words of affirmation" it is quite humbling for me to read the following and, frankly, in a few cases, I actually got a tad emotional perusing each author's perception of my skill set. Many thanks and much appreciation go to all who took the time to review for me their experiences in hiring me to present at national and/or state conferences or attending same. I look forward to doing many more while meeting in person many of you who have honored me by reading my freshman project you're now holding in your hands

---

"Quality training comes in many forms. It may be determined by training topic content, skills of the trainer, depth of knowledge on the topic, etc. An element that is sometimes forgotten is the emotion shared by the trainer. Kim Combes not only provides all of the qualities normally referred to as a quality trainer but he adds the genuine element of emotion to his presentations. You know he is completely engaged and feeling each and every word he is sharing. This makes for a most impactful learning experience and keeps people coming back for more.

Speaking Endorsements

Lived experiences added to educational attainment in a specific field improves the quality of the learning experience. Trusting the trainer is key to absorbing the content of the information. Kim quickly engages his audience with his caring and non-threatening approach. His lived experiences enhance his ability to "speak" in terms and feelings that others can easily understand and relate to on any given day.

Kim has presented workshops many times to two organizations I am close to – the National Foster Parent Association and the Texas Foster Family Association. Each year we are asked if Kim will be speaking at our annual conferences.

Kim shares relevant information that caregivers and workers need as they struggle to meet the needs of the children and families they serve in the foster care systems across this country."

— *Irene Clements, NFPA, Executive Director; TFFA Content Expert; NCTSN Advisory Board; SAFE Coalition for Human Rights Board of Directors*

"It is my pleasure and honor to recommend Mr. Kim Combes for his outstanding training skills. Mr. Combes approaches training with a passion strengthened through his vast personal experiences with child welfare as a professional counselor and as a foster and adoptive father. His sound child welfare knowledge and his strong foundation of personal values inform his professional work.

When I met Kim years ago, I was impressed at how quickly and personably he engaged with me. Engagement is a quality that defines Kim. He cares for people and wants to understand them deeply. He uses that quality in his training to bring out the best qualities in his audiences.

In addition to his engagement skills, Kim brings an energy to his training that keeps participants alert and ready to be part of the discussion and learning. I have seen Kim in action during many workshops and each time I was happy and excited to be there.

When I was the national training development director for the Child Welfare Institute we contracted with Kim to develop a training guide for foster parents focused on managing anger. Kim has a keen sense of how to organize training so that participants learn in comfortable and sequential steps.

Simply put, Kim Combes is a terrific child welfare trainer!"

— *Heather Craig-Oldsen, MSW, Professor of Social Work (retired) Briar Cliff University; National Presenter*

Walk In A Manner Worthy

"I have known Kim Combes since 2009. He is the principle developer for one of our national curricula titled "Shared Parenting: Helping Children in Foster Care Manage Anger." Kim trained Kansas trainers on how to deliver that training and another one called "Beyond Consequences". The participants raved about his workshop. He brought knowledge and expertise to the training. He is dedicated to making a difference in the lives of children who have experienced traumatic events. He not only shares his ideas, he spreads the passion to help children and families."
— *Denise Gibson, Director of National Programs, Children's Alliance of Kansas*

Thank you for the opportunity to support Kim Combes' continuing work and growth in social services, child welfare, and training.

I have known Kim for 30 years in his role as a social worker, trainer, and foster/adoptive parent.

During my time as Executive Director of the Iowa Foster and Adoptive Parents Association (IFAPA), we contracted with Kim to develop and deliver training statewide and at our annual conferences for foster/adopt/kinship families and workers. He does an outstanding job in relating to the families and workers. He shares his experiences and mistakes as a foster/adoptive parent for others to learn from them.

Kim's classes were one of the most sought after classes. The foster/adopt/kinship families feel comfortable and eager to learn because he reflects solid parenting techniques and practices. In his work Kim understands and follows social work values and ethics, along with his strong personal values.

These following comments are from some of the families at our IFAPA trainings. These comments are the best testimonials to his talent, passion, knowledge, ability to relate, and advocacy for all in the child welfare systems. — *Lynhon Stout, Former Executive Director of Iowa Foster/Adoptive Parent Association*

"I have attended workshops that Kim has done, both on a local and national level. Kim does an awesome job of engaging the audience, giving much needed information and touching each person in a personal way. I highly recommend Kim!"
— *Pamela Allen, Former Director of Nebraska Foster/Adoptive Parent Association*

Speaking Endorsements

"I have had the pleasure of knowing Kim Combes for many years. In the past, the Nebraska Foster & Adoptive Parent Association conducted several foster conferences every year. Kim was always open to possibilities of presenting keynotes and workshops and discussed with us what might work better based on the objectives for our conference. In addition, he even developed a training that we wanted to showcase since the issue was becoming more prominent in Nebraska.

Kim relates well with foster and adoptive parents because he has gone through the issues they are facing. He is able to bring his knowledge, experience, recommendations and ideas to help foster and adoptive parents with the children in their home. His ability to relate with them is what really makes him an amazing presenter. Many people would stop me at the conferences to tell me how amazing and inspirational he is. This is why we always asked him back to conferences! See below some of the comments from evaluations we received from his workshops/keynotes. I would highly recommend Kim for keynotes and workshops that will be relevant, useful and inspirational. We look forward to having him come back to Nebraska soon. The following are some of his evaluation comments:

- Very good speaker.
- Enjoy him every time!
- Good personal experience stories. Excellent!
- Kim has a lot of knowledge-wish I could spend much more time with him. Good resources presented.
- He knows his stuff. Great information and kept us going with the q and a.
- Interesting, stimulating, thought-provoking and sharing interactively.
- Relates well with audience. A lot of good points to make you think what you could change and do.
- Kim provided humor and evidence-based facts in his presentation. Good resources.
- So real!
- Kim's stories are relevant and inspirational.
- Excellent and unassuming presence. Focused and to the point. Would like to hear more from him.
- Hope I can be as supportive and strong when a child of mine wants to do this.
- Helpful for us regarding our adopted sons.
- Pleasant attitude and personality. Please invite back."

— *Felicia Nelsen, Executive Director of Nebraska Foster/Adoptive Parent Association*

Walk In A Manner Worthy

"For many years I have known Kim as a colleague, trainer, and friend. I have always appreciated his approach to behavior management from both theoretical and practical perspective. Kim has proven himself over the years as an advocate for all in the Foster Care/Adoption system and beyond." – *Ruthann Jarrett, Retired Foster Care/Adoption Coordinator – Children and Families of Iowa (CFI)*

Engaging, knowledgeable, humorous, using REAL life examples and heartfelt passion: these are just a few of the words to describe the awesome presentation given by Mr. Kim Combes sharing the Nurtured Heart Approach to my staff and volunteers and our community at large. I could feel the crowd energy come alive at the prospect of having guidance to make a true shift in perspective and "how to's" focusing on the positive characteristics in difficult relationships to make them juicy and peaceful. Although it will take practice and focused energy to accomplish this shift consistently, the evaluations showed it was practical for relating to children through geriatric situations. There continues to be reference to the learning even weeks after the training. Thank you, Kim, for infusing energy and hope for weary educators, social workers and hospice caregivers through the learning, laughter and tears you provided through this training.

Celeste Eld, Executive Director, Hospice of Eastern Idaho

We always enjoy attending trainings and classes presented by Kim Combes. He always leads a great training and you come away feeling more confident as a foster parent, mother/father and as a family. Kim is always able to show real life examples of the concepts he teaches. He is able show us how to apply these ideas and techniques to your everyday struggles. I highly recommend Kim for training and speaking obligations.—*EJ and Amber Bell*

Just wanted to thank you again for having us at the training! We have done our best to implement the Nurtured Heart Approach. It's been so good for our family! Our kids are SOOO much more willing to respond well. I can tell they feel more loved which has produced better attitudes for everyone and I see more love between the 3 of them. My oldest son has responded GREAT and I can count the true problems with him on my fingers since attending your training. Thanks again for teaching and equipping others! – *Alyssa and Josh Hulme*

Speaking Endorsements

"I observed Kim presenting a 6 hour training through the Iowa Foster/Adoptive Parent Association (IFAPA) titled: "The Nurtured Heart Approach". Kim was at all times attentive to the group in which he was teaching, he kept them engaged and interacting, and was personable. Kim allowed for questions and was very good at politely keeping the group on task. I would recommend him highly as I would sit through a class of his again with no hesitation." — *Rachel Kalpin*

"We heard Kim speak at our very first IFAPA conference 3½ years ago! We were so very touched by his story of going from a social worker, to foster parent and then to adoptive parent! Too, we were touched then to meet two of his sons! It was so incredible to see and hear how God worked in his life and the lives of his kids! We had a long battle with infertility ourselves! It was Kim's story that inspired us to become licensed foster parents and not give up on the dream of having our own family! We got licensed a few months after that conference and started our own journey from fostering to a forever family! We just adopted our two boys on June 26th of this year and are blessed beyond belief to have these amazing kids in our family!!! Thanks!"— Sara Bengfort

---

"I have attended several IFAPA trainings led by Kim Combes. His presentations on attachment and therapeutic parenting approaches were full of practical ideas and advice. His life experience as a foster/adoptive parent and professional experience in the field of social work provided a unique insight. He was well equipped to talk about constructive ways to navigate the challenges of parenting children from hard places. His training on "Nurtured Heart Approach" was especially beneficial to our family. His passion for the subject matter came through in his presentation. The knowledge we gained from the training helped us adjust many of our parenting techniques. It has helped us break down barriers and develop a deep connectedness with our children." *Deb Barry*

"Kim Combes is THE best speaker/trainer we ever had while being foster parents in Iowa! Being foster parents for 10 years and going through 6 hours of training each year, enabled us to hear many speakers. Kim's classes were very down-to-earth and practical! He always challenged us to become better at helping the many hurting hearts that passed through our home! Although we are no longer foster parents, we would still jump at any opportunity to hear him speak. The wisdom he shares is profitable for daily life!" — *Jesse and Rhonda Bullard*

"My husband and I took an IFAPA class for our foster parent license from Kim Combes and learned so much! The class was "Healing the Heart of a Challenging Child." Kim made the class interesting, informative, and fun! Kim loves people, you can tell by the way he interacts with everyone in the class! We would highly recommend Kim Combes as an educator, counselor, author, or any other way Kim could reach people!" — *Ron and Diane Gasteiger*

"Raising children today is a challenge but often even more so for foster/adopt parents. "Why is my child doing this?" Kim has years of practical experience and is willing to tackle the hard issues that others won't. His presentations are engaging, relevant and well worth attending." — *Byron and Pam Keefe*

"I participated in a federal foster care review yesterday in Des Moines. The federal agents asked a lot of questions about trainings. Every single family raved about how amazing your trainings are. And how foster homes are specifically seeking out your classes to take. Your classes have touched more hearts, and helped more families and kids than you know. I thought you should know. You are doing amazing things for our families!!! We were unanimous in saying that you are the top educator in our area. Two people were crying. That is how much you meant to them and how much you actually changed their lives. And mine. Thank you!!" — *Hattie Potter Salmonson*

VITA FOR MR. KIM COMBES, M.Ed.

EDUCATIONAL BACKGROUND:

B.A. in psychology/sociology from Westmar College in LeMars, IA. - May, 1980

M.Ed degree in Counselor Education from Iowa State University in Ames, IA. - 3.66 G.P.A. - May, 2003

EMPLOYMENT HISTORY:

In-home worker (part-time) for Life Connections headquartered in Cedar Rapids, IA. September 2010 - March 2012

Therapist for Beloit (Lutheran Services in Iowa) in Ames, IA. January 2006 - January 2007

Case Manager for Story County Community Services in Ames, IA. July 2004- January 2006

Family Therapist for Quakerdale in New Providence, IA. June 2003-March 2005

Combes Counseling and Consultation (counseling/trainings/presentations) in Colo, IA. July 1994-Present

Treatment foster and/or adoptive parent for Iowa Department of Human Services in Story County, IA. May 1994-Present

Family-centered services and foster care specialist for Lutheran Social Service in Ames, IA. August 1994-June 1997

Foster care training specialist II at Iowa State University in Ames, IA. March 1989-July 1994

Human Service Agencies (Beloit, Ames Community High School, Iowa Dept of Human Services) June 1980- March 1989

NATIONAL TRAINING EXPERIENCE:

Presented workshops for community colleges, churches, youth groups, and other conferences nationally and statewide

Presented workshops at 13 national conferences: Chicago (1993); St. Petersburg,

(1994); Grand Rapids (1994); San Antonio (1998); Minneapolis (2000); Cincinnati (2001); Las Vegas (2002); Des Moines (2003); Orlando (2004); Los Angeles (2005); San Antonio (2006); Wash. DC (2007); and Des Moines (2008).

EXTENDED EDUCATIONAL CREDITS
Certified National Foster Parent Association (NFPA) Trainer 2001.
Wrote training curriculum for Child Welfare Institute of Atlanta, GA., 2002.
Certified to facilitate Family Team Meetings since February 2000.
Trained, too, in mediation services in June 2001 and the Red Cross's Critical Incident Stress Management in November 2001 as well as training in the Mandt System Anger De-Escalation Training, August 2006.
Certified in February 2006 by Nancy Thomas to train "Parenting Challenging Children".
Certified National Presenter for Gurian Institute in Colorado Springs, CO. July, 2007.
Joined NFPA Speaker's Bureau in January 2008.
Certified Trainer for Promoting Social Emotional Competence and Strengthening Families Program 10-14 in June 2008.
Bryan Post Institute Training in May 2009.
Wrote curriculum for Children's Alliance of Kansas January 2010.
Psychological First Aid and Critical Incident Stress Management certified in September 2010. Mentoring for Violence Prevention training 2012.
Two-day training Caring for Children Who Have Experienced Trauma Educational Forum August 2013.

Nurtured Heart Approach Certified Trainer August 2014. It's Not About You training September 2014. Connection Matters 2015. Wonderfully Made Family Camp board member November 2015-Present.

OTHER ACTIVITIES:

Youth Group Leader for two groups (7-12 grade) at Cornerstone Church of Christ in Zearing, IA. (2008-2017)

- Colo-Nesco High School Advisory Committee (1998-1999) Bullying Prevention Program at CN Middle School (2007-2011)

Iowa Child and Family Services Stakeholder Panel (2008-2010) Iowa Trauma Informed Care Stakeholder Panel (2012-Present)

Vita For Mr Combes

National Foster Parent Association Board Member [Nominations Chairperson] (2000-2003) [Region 7 Vice-President] (2003-2005)

President of the Story County Foster Parent Association (1998-2004) Story County Empowerment Board Member (1999-2003)

Iowa Foster/Adoptive Parent Association Board Member (IFAPA) [Regional Representative/VP] (2000-2003)

Published writer in issues of ADOPTION TODAY, ROOTS AND WINGS ADOPTION MAGAZINE, NFPA NATIONAL ADVOCATE along with various other articles in local publications and professional magazines/blogs. Currently an Advisory Board member and regular columnist for the quarterly FOSTERING FAMILIES TODAY magazine. Too, I contributed a piece to the college textbook, BRIEF THERAPY IN ACTION by Dr. John Littrell, REMBRANDT REMEMBERS : 80 YEARS OF SMALL TOWN LIFE an Iowa Historical Society award-winning anthology, and to THE FOSTER PARENTING TOOLBOX and THE KINSHIP PARENTING TOOLBOX edited by Kim Phagan-Hansel.

MR. M. KIM COMBES, DIRECTOR OF COMBES COUNSELING AND CONSULTATION

406 West Street   Colo, IA. 50056   515-291-4014 (C)   kcombes@netins.net

Walk In A Manner Worthy